Training for
Total Quality Management

The Kogan Page Practical Trainer Series

Series Editor: Roger Buckley

PRACTICAL TRAINER SERIES

Training for
Total Quality Management

DAVID R JEFFRIES   BILL EVANS   PETER REYNOLDS

KOGAN PAGE
Published in association with the
Institute of Training and Development

First published in 1992
Reprinted 1993

Kogan Page Limited
120 Pentonville Road
London N1 9JN

© David R. Jeffries, Bill Evans, Peter Reynolds, 1992, 1993

British Library Cataloguing in Publication Data

A CIP record for this book is available from the British Library.

ISBN 0 7494 0754 9

Typeset by Koinonia Ltd, Bury
Printed and bound in Great Britain by
Biddles Ltd, Guildford and King's Lynn

Contents

Series Editor's Foreword

Organizations get things done when people do their jobs effectively. To make this happen they need to be well trained. A number of people are likely to be involved in this training by identifying the needs of the organization and of the individual, by selecting or designing appropriate training to meet those needs, by delivering it and assessing how effective it was. It is not only 'professional' or full-time trainers who are involved in this process; personnel managers, line managers, supervisors and job holders are all likely to have a part to play.

This series has been written for all those who get involved with training in some way or another, whether they are senior personnel managers trying to link the goals of the organization with training needs or job holders who have been given responsibility for training newcomers. Therefore, the series is essentially a practical one which focuses on specific aspects of the training function. This book is the 12th to be published in the series which has become so popular that it is intended to include additional volumes whenever a need is found for practical guidelines in some area of training. This is not to say that the theoretical underpinnings of the practical aspects of training are unimportant. Anyone seriously interested in training is strongly encouraged to look beyond 'what to do' and 'how to do it' and to delve into the areas of why things are done in a particular way.

The authors have been selected because they have considerable practical experience. All have shared, at some time, the same difficulties, frustrations and satisfactions of being involved in training and are now in a position to share with others some helpful and practical guidelines.

In this book the authors show how the role of the trainer impacts on the broader aspects of organizational change and development. Over recent years the demands on trainers have increased as it has become recognized that they have those skills that enable them, often better than others, to influence and to guide change.

Total Quality Management is one of those areas in which trainers can have considerable impact. TQM is about improving performance to meet customer demands and to improve every aspect of an organization's activities. Improved performance is what training and development are all about. This book guides trainers through the activities in which they will have to become involved in order to implement a TQM initiative. It illustrates those skills that they will have to employ in working as an internal consultant alongside managers to clarify the organization's vision, to facilitate learning, to encourage and to implement change.

ROGER BUCKLEY

Preface

Training for Total Quality Management has been written with three specific groups of people in mind:

- trainers and training officers who are involved with TQM or who wish to learn more about how training can contribute to TQM;
- training consultants and TQM consultants;
- TQM executives or directors/senior managers who have a responsibility for implementing TQM in their organization.

In writing the book we sought to:

- provide a working model of the TQM process;
- provide detailed information about how TQM can be implemented;
- provide detailed information on how the reader can help facilitate change in their own organization.

Within the text the word 'customer' is of crucial importance. In TQM the concept of the 'customer' is much wider than in normal usage where it refers to people who eventually buy a product or service – they are usually the recipients in a commercial transaction. However, within TQM this is not always the case. The patient in a hospital or student in a school may not pay directly for the service they receive but they are still customers who deserve a quality service. TQM is therefore just as relevant in these organizations as it is in any manufacturing or commercial concern. In many respects this extension of the word customer is easy to accept. Regardless of whether money changes hands, customers are simply people who are external to the organization who receive the product or service which the organization has to offer. Yet in TQM the concept of customer is extended still further.

Many people in organizations never come into contact with the external customer. Take for example the lab assistant in a hospital or the caretaker in a school. In the normal course of events they are unlikely to have any direct contact with external customers. Yet their work is crucial for the wider organization to succeed. Despite the fact that they do not meet the external customer they do provide essential services for other people within the organization. In TQM this is recognized by acknowledging that they serve internal customers. Indeed in the TQM organization everyone is committed to providing both internal and external customers with quality service.

As a trainer, it is also important that you are customer-centred in your approach to training. If you think for a moment you will probably recognize that you serve a wide range of different customers. They will include people who attend your formal training programmes, managers and supervisors throughout your organization, your Board of Directors, indeed anyone who seeks your help and advice (either internal or external). They all deserve a quality training service and we hope this book will help you fulfil that role.

That fact that in TQM the word 'customer' has several slightly different meanings has given us some problems in writing the book. Sometimes we have used the word to refer to the external customer, sometimes it refers to internal customers within the organization, and at other times we have used it to refer specifically to the customers of training. However, when using these different meanings we have tried to make it clear in the text precisely who we mean.

It is also important to say a few words about how the book is structured. Chapter 1 provides an overview of TQM in general, highlighting distinct operational areas which may need attention if TQM is to succeed. Subsequent chapters then address each of these areas from the trainer's viewpoint. As you will see, in each case we have tried to emphasize what the trainer can do to move his/her organization forward.

Within the book you will note that the sections of each chapter are based on a series of questions. This is because we believe that the TQM training role is often about asking questions and then helping people discover appropriate answers. The main body of text which follows provides answers to the questions. Our choice of which questions to address has been based on the types of questions which participants raise during our training events about 'Training and TQM'. The answers and explanations we have given are drawn from our experience of working with many organizations who are adopting TQM. We hope this is sufficiently thorough for the reader to feel able to apply the ideas in their own company.

Finally, it is also worth mentioning that the book is laid out sequentially, with each chapter dealing with a specific aspect of TQM. All of the topics mentioned are important, but in practice they will rarely be applied in such a uniform and sequential manner. Different organizations will need a different emphasis and approach for each area, depending on individual organizational circumstances. For the trainer (or consultant) this provides a challenging and stimulating working environment.

TQM is no passing fad. For the trainer it offers the opportunity, perhaps for the first time, to design and participate in training initiatives which involve and affect the whole organization. In our view training is essential. It is the only service which can help companies adopt all of the changes which TQM demands.

Acknowledgements

As with most books, many people have been involved over the years helping shape and guide our thinking to the point where writing this text became possible. However, a few deserve special mention. Firstly we would like to pay a special tribute to Robert Hart, a friend and colleague. Without his invaluable tutoring this book would never have materialized. Secondly, we must mention Tony Kniveton and Lorna McClure for their help and contributions. Thanks also to Tom Dudding for his generous artistic support and Alix Horne and Barbara Humphries for their hours typing and retyping without complaint.

Finally, to our wives Susan, Marion and Barbara (and children) we owe a debt of thanks for their tolerance and support. Their interest and encouragement is beyond value.

1 TQM, An Overview

▷   S U M M A R Y   ◁

- Total Quality Management is a comprehensive and integrated way of managing any organization in order to:
  a) meet the needs of the customer consistently
  b) achieve continuous improvement in every aspect of the organization's activities.
- Quality is determined by the customer; use it to your advantage or ignore it at your peril.
- TQM is a journey towards the company's vision.
- Goal clarity is absolutely essential at all levels of the organization.
- Measures must be used to reflect progress/improvement.
- Measure your service or product the same way as the customer does.
- Know what your customer wants, don't assume you know. Customers' needs change, you must change with them (or slightly ahead of them).
- Continuous improvement embraces doing a job right first time.

TQM, What is It?

Imagine a company where: 'The customer is more important than the boss'. An obvious enough statement to make and probably one to which most bosses would give their support. And yet too often we find that 'keeping the boss happy' becomes the be all and end all for employees often to the detriment of the customer. TQM changes this.

Imagine a company where: 'People come up with ideas not excuses'. How often have we heard, 'That will never work', or 'Ah yes but...', or

'Once you've worked here as long as I have mate you'll know', or 'I've heard some rubbish in my day but that suggestion is ridiculous'. These blocking, excuse-making statements not only prevent improvement but also kill off future creativity. TQM changes this.

Imagine a company where: 'Fear is replaced by trust'. So much fear exists in so many organizations. Fear of failure, fear of looking a fool, fear of the sack, fear of being singled out, fear of having a black mark, fear of being wrong. Such strong negative feelings in the workplace achieve very little of any value. TQM changes this.

Imagine a company where: 'Power is replaced by accountability'. In traditionally-run organizations the higher up the management ladder you are the more power you have, and you hold onto it. With TQM power is handed back down as necessary to ensure that the job gets done.

Imagine a company where: 'Difficult issues are on the agenda'. We have found from working with various clients that meetings at all levels in the organization tend to start with performance, targets, budgets, etc and frequently, and some may say conveniently, time runs out before the difficult issues are dealt with. By this we refer to the way people work together – issues like morale, participation, feelings of trust and mistrust, internal cooperation instead of internal competition. TQM changes this.

Imagine a company where: 'Delivery and performance are more important than authority'. Customers want service, accuracy, quality, competitive pricing. These are some of the things important to them. What helps a company ensure the customer gets these things and more, is having processes developed precisely for this purpose. Who's in charge isn't usually part of this equation!

Imagine a company where: 'Trainers make a real impact'. With TQM, training is clearly geared to achieve one thing and that is improving performance! Trainers who live this message become an intrinsic, difficult to replace, valued part of the organization which they serve.

These represent some of the characteristics which are addressed and dealt with by TQM. So what do we mean by TQM? There is no right answer to the question. We use a fairly simple definition:

> Total Quality Management is a comprehensive and integrated way of managing any organization in order to:
> a)   meet the needs of the customer consistently
> b)   achieve continuous improvement in every aspect of the organization's activities.

> **TRAINER'S TIP**
>
> If senior management are serious about TQM they need to spend some time working on their own answer to the question: 'What does TQM mean for us?' If they start with their own definition then they are more likely to be committed to it. You also need to spend some time developing your own answer.

As a Trainer Where do I Fit in?

TQM is fundamentally about change. For some organizations this may be very slight perhaps only shifting the emphasis. For other organizations the change may be massive. Inevitably culture and management style will be high on the agenda. In addition the organization's information systems, control systems, management and operational procedures will also be affected. New skills will be necessary – project skills, customer contact skills, behavioural skills, structural skills... The list goes on. The one common denominator is always people.

The trainer has a central role to play in this change process. As this book is devoted to looking at TQM from a trainer's perspective (and this also includes consultants and other TQM helpers), it seems appropriate to list here the main features of the role of the trainer:

- To initially build commitment with the senior management team and establish clarity of purpose, ie the vision.
- To develop a good conceptual understanding of TQM and be able to interpret this into the framework and language of your own organization.
- To have a high profile alongside managers as, through a 'Cascade Approach', you develop people's understanding of TQM.
- To be a resource in terms of developing appropriate training packages.
- To be a deliverer of training.
- To resource, either directly or indirectly, training that is required.
- To work as an internal consultant to line managers. This is their initiative not yours.
- To help managers and employees alike to address behavioural and relationship difficulties.
- To facilitate effective communication and interaction across and within departments.

- To encourage and develop accountability throughout the organization.
- To be a good role model.
- Be a conscience to the organization. Be prepared to confront any inconsistencies between what has been agreed as good TQM practice and behaviour in the business and what people actually do.

Why Total Quality Management?

The business climate of today is one of continually rising customer expectations. Satisfying these expectations which businesses, companies and organizations need to do to survive, serves only to raise customer expectations even higher. Businesses need to be able to respond and meet these continually rising expectations. Reason? Simple! If you don't meet these needs then someone else will.

You and your organization might think that you have loyal customers, they've been with you for years and you're sure they will remain so. This might be true; however our research would suggest that this is a big and dangerous assumption to make. Customers of today, be they the general public, the high street retailer or another organization or company, more often than not expect and demand high standards in whichever shape or form *they* choose it to be. In other words, Quality with a capital Q is determined by the Customer with a capital C. We need to respond and meet these customers needs and requirements. These are the realities of the market-based economy in which we live. It is a reality where the customer is king, where the customer selects and decides what they want and then finds someone who will give it to them.

For many organizations there is increasing competition from all corners of the world which needs to be contended with. This only reinforces the fact that to survive, grow, be profitable, offer employment to others, and be perceived as world leaders in your respective fields, you need to adopt a policy and practice of meeting the needs of the customer and of achieving continuous improvement.

Here quality as determined and specified by the customer is a major strategic issue. Use it to your advantage or ignore it at your peril!

Perhaps there may still be exceptions to this scenario, where the customer is not so demanding. In these situations the supplier, provider or vendor to a greater degree determines what the customer can have. The classic example of this was in the early days of the Ford car empire, when Ford announced that 'you can have any colour you want as long as it is black'. With the exception of low volume special editions, how successful do you think this approach would be today? Where these companies do exist, we would suggest that they are few and far between and rapidly becoming extinct! It is only a matter of time, in a market-based economy, before the customers say, 'enough is enough' and start to become more demanding by exerting the power and influence that is rightly theirs.

Organizations which have compliant, undemanding customers should be using this breathing space to shape up their act as their honeymoon is about to end. Most companies are already contending with high customer expectations as well as competing with both domestic and overseas competition. As a result, and as shown in Figure 1.1, the lifeblood of business – cash and profit – is under threat.

Customer Requirement   Other Pressures

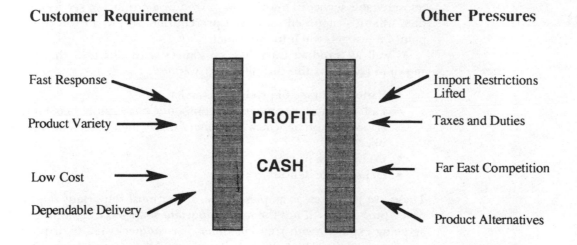

Figure 1.1 *Business pressures*

It also needs to be recognized that governments often add further pressures by introducing new legislation or lifting or removing legislation such as import restrictions. In fairness, however, it can also be argued that these actions are themselves part of a market-based economy and are designed to encourage growth, economic health and commercial longevity by getting managers to focus on running their companies as effectively as possible under real as opposed to artificially created market conditions.

The nub of this customer-based pressure is that *to be competitive, profitable and enjoy the PRIVILEGE of continuing to supply customers with goods and services you need to adopt a policy and practice of Total Quality Management.*

19

> ### TRAINER'S TIP
>
> A useful activity at the 'front end' of any TQM initiative is for the senior managers to apply the same process as shown in Figure 1.1 to their own business. To do this simply ask them to list the customer requirements and other external pressures which they believe the organization is working under.

Quality as Determined by the Customer – What does this Mean?

There used to be a time when you could advertise your product or service as being of the 'highest·standard of manufacture' or 'will last for ever' or 'most reliable service in town'. Now, providing a product or service which does what it's supposed to do is a prerequisite. It doesn't win you any points, it just gets you into the game!

As well as 'product integrity', customers want different things. As shown in Figure 1.1 the customer here wants:

- Variety or range of product or service.
- Faster response (time-based competition is rapidly becoming a critical factor by which customers make their selection of supplier).
- Competitive pricing.
- Dependable delivery.

These are just a few examples. One of the most important stages of developing TQM – if not the most important stage – is establishing and agreeing explicitly with your customer or customers what their precise requirements are. This will be the starting point for developing a TQM organization.

Definition of Quality

If we were to compare two cars, say a Mercedes Benz and a Mini, (Figure 1.2) which is the quality car?

Answer: they both are.

Why? Simple! If you had a potential customer who was looking for a vehicle which would: be handy just for running down to the shops; be easy to park; be economical to run; seats three and a dog in relative comfort; be inexpensive; be inexpensive to service – the Mini meets these requirements and therefore by definition is a quality car.

On the other hand if you have someone who wants a car which will be

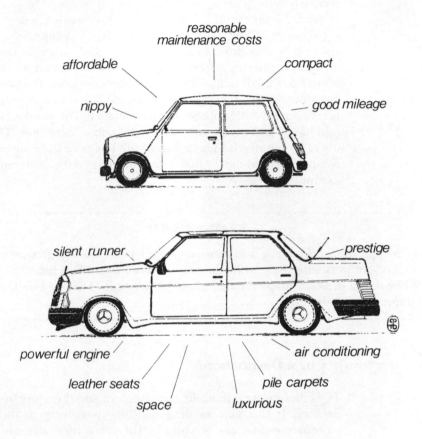

reasonable
maintenance costs

affordable

compact

nippy

good mileage

silent runner

prestige

powerful engine

air conditioning

leather seats

pile carpets

space

luxurious

COMPARISON OF QUALITY

Figure 1.2 *Comparison of Quality*

air-conditioned; have luxurious upholstery; provide the ultimate in in-car entertainment; impress passengers and observers alike; run silently at high speeds – then the Mercedes Benz meets these requirements and therefore can be regarded as a quality car.

So, when we define quality we know that it is determined by the customer. However, we need to be careful that we do not confuse luxury with quality. Consequently, you may find it helpful to consider product or service quality as being 'fit for purpose' as required by the customer.

With the car example it is easy to see how quality as determined by the customer is strategically very important, as compliance with this will either take you closer to securing a sale and satisfying the customer or take you further away from it. Again, use it to your advantage or ignore it at your peril! For many businesses, their customer may not be the actual consumer or product user. For example, a fast moving consumer goods manufacturer will probably sell to a retailer. The product will in turn be purchased and consumed or used by a final customer. Therefore your organization needs to be aware of the needs of the customer chain and respond accordingly. Quality as determined by customers is of paramount importance.

TRAINER'S TIP

Pose the question, 'What do our customers want from us?' to groups of senior managers and work with them while they agree a comprehensive list.

While doing this encourage them to identify the needs of the end user, as well as the immediate customer.

TQM – is it a Journey or a Destination?

TQM embraces continuous improvement and therefore by definition is a journey. It is a journey or a continuous striving to meet ever-rising customer requirements whilst at the same time achieving continuous improvement in every aspect of the organization's operations. TQM is a means to an end, the end being the organization's mission, vision or goal (see Figure 1.3)

Figure 1.3 *The vision – the starting point for TQM*

We will discuss the vision in detail in Chapter 3. It is important at this stage to emphasize that *goal clarity* is absolutely essential to ensure that all activities within the organization are aligned and moving the organization in the same direction, that of achieving the vision.

Part of the trainer's role with TQM is asking the question and getting others to ask the question continuously:

If we do this, will it take us closer to or further away from the vision?

Our experience with various organizations has led us to conclude that this is a very powerful diagnostic question. Of course, to get sensible replies requires everyone in the organization to know what the vision is!

TRAINER'S TIP

Keep asking people: 'How does this activity take the organization closer to the vision and if it doesn't, why are you doing it?'

How can we Measure our Progress?

The measures used must reflect the content of the vision covering areas such as

- Customer satisfaction
- Profitability/Performance
- Product/Service Quality
- Valuing Employees

In addition, the measures need to reflect progress/improvement in all of these areas. Recording, monitoring and measuring performance improvement is an essential feature of any Total Quality drive. Departments, teams and individuals need to know how well they are doing, how much progress has been made, how close to the goal or vision they are. For this to be possible explicit performance targets must be agreed and established *at all levels* in the organization. The concept of measuring will be discussed in much greater detail in Chapter 5.

Once the vision has been established it is likely that distinct areas such as those shown in Figure 1.4 will need to become the focus for measurement. We shall briefly look at each area now, although more in-depth analysis will follow in the relevant chapters.

Figure 1.4 *Components of the vision*

1. Measuring Customer Satisfaction and Company Profitability

Customer satisfaction and company profitability are inexorably linked together. If you don't satisfy customers, you lose them and this has an adverse effect on profit. Profit has traditionally been a key indication of success and rightly so. Banks, shareholders and the City usually act and react on an organization's financial performance of which profit is a key factor. It can also be argued that one of the greatest disservices an organization can do for its employees is not to make a profit.

So with TQM profitability is an important measure. What is of equal importance is customer satisfaction. Question: How do you measure customer satisfaction? Answer: The same way in which the customer does! You already know that quality is determined by the customer and that your organization needs to have clearly agreed customer requirements (or business order-winning criteria). These are the yardsticks by which you are measured by the customer. Therefore these are the characteristics and dimensions which must be monitored and measured. If currently your data system cannot give this information, then you will need to change your system!

To give an example of this. One organization we worked with regarded themselves as being a good supplier of their particular product. They paid meticulous attention to product quality (integrity); their prices were competitive; their employees were very courteous to the customer; and they consistently achieved excellent delivery date accuracy. And yet they were surprised when they found out that two out of three of their major customers regarded them as only satisfactory to poor and the third customer as only satisfactory! Why did the customers see them like this? Simple! Their order-to-delivery cycle time was a disaster. It hadn't improved in two and a half years. The company had not stayed close enough to its customers to find out that in that period, the customers' business order-winning criteria had changed!

TRAINER'S TIP

To measure customer satisfaction requires talking to the customer and finding out:
- What do they want?
- How will they measure you?
- How well you are doing and then doing it better!

---

2. Measuring Continuous Operation Improvement

To give an insight into what is meant here, consider a traditional or non-TQM organization; this could apply equally in services, retail, the public sector or manufacturing.

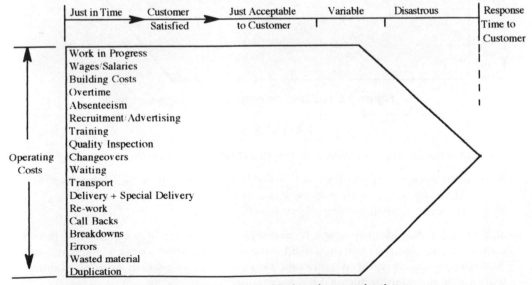

Figure 1.5 *The fat and lethargic organization*

Figure 1.5 shows an organization which is 'fat' as depicted by all the contributing factors under operating costs and also 'lethargic', represented by this being a long arrow rather than a short one. As you can see the horizontal axis (response time) is sectioned into degrees of responsiveness. As mentioned earlier in this chapter, time-based competition is rapidly becoming a critical factor in winning and retaining customers, therefore the shorter the arrow, the more effective you are generally both for the customer and your own company. The intention with TQM is to significantly reduce the operating costs and the response times in accordance with customer requirements. This is represented in Figure 1.6.

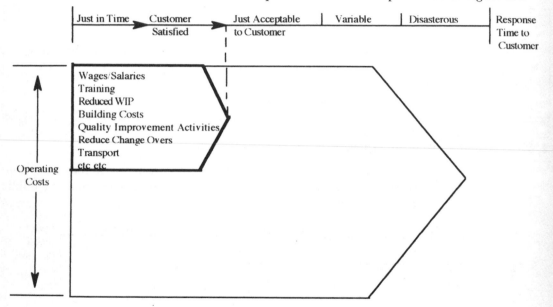

Figure 1.6 *The lean, hungry and fast organization*

TRAINER'S TIP

We find it useful to get managers to use this model to identify:

a) their component operating costs of the business as well as the elements which lengthen the response time to the customer;

b) the response time of the organization as they see it.

In Figure 1.7 they identify how it is currently, in Figure 1.8 they can identify how it could be. The managers will then need some help to develop a strategy to move from 'the current' to 'the desired' situation. This exercise can usefully be applied either within a department or across the organization.

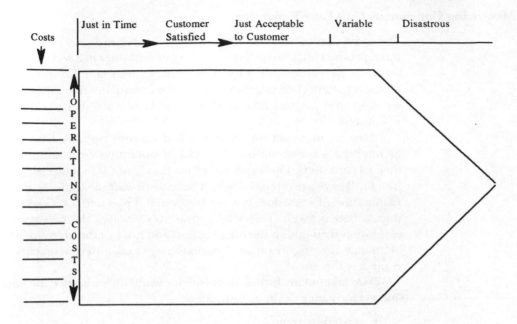

Figure 1.7 *My organization – how it is now*

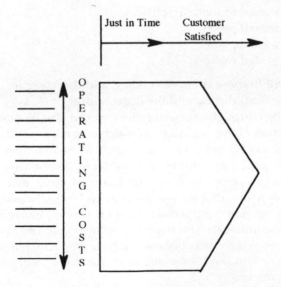

Figure 1.8 *My organization – how it could be*

3. Measuring Continuous Unit Cost Reduction

The reduction of unit cost (and by this we refer not only to a manufactured product but also the average cost per customer in a service environment) is of paramount importance. It is important for everyone in business to have clear targets to work to (be careful not to set these targets too low) and performance against these targets needs to be regularly monitored.

There are many activities which will affect unit cost. We have already highlighted a two-dimensional model of operating costs and response time to customers. Obviously the effort that is put into addressing these issues will have a profound effect. The issue of waste also affects unit cost. Elimination of waste does not just happen, it is planned for. Goals are set then action is taken. This action invariably involves the managers and employees throughout the organization and not just the accountant who often may move figures around so that things look different on paper but really stay the same!

Waste takes many forms, all of which eventually influence the bottom line performance of the organization:

- wasted material
- wasted space
- wasted time
- wasted movement/effort
- wasted power
- wasted plant
- wasted cash

These all become issues of concern and therefore legitimate targets for improvement throughout the organization.

Savings through unit cost reduction can also be made by focusing on those areas of the organization which cost money with no return on the investment. We refer to aspects such as errors, mistakes and re-work. TQM is aimed at considerably reducing, to the point of theoretically eliminating, errors. Anyone who has read other material on TQM will probably realize that many organizations 'shoot themselves in the foot' by employing quality inspectors. By their very existence quality inspectors often communicate a message to employees, that we as a company expect people to make errors because we have inspectors here to inspect these errors out and then someone, somewhere else, will probably re-work or correct the errors.

This is not to say that some inspection in certain processes is not critical, but even given this caveat, there is still a lot of scope for reducing the amount of designated inspectors whilst at the same time increasing individual accountability. *Individual and team accountability is the primary route to the elimination of errors*, or, 'zero defect', as it has come to be known. There is much discussion on the question of whether 'zero defect' is a commercially realistic target to aim for. We will stay out of that intellectual debate, but still conclude this point by saying error reduction, ie people doing the job right first time, is demonstrably a cost reduction activity.

It is essential that the quest for continuous unit cost reduction is approached on at least three separate fronts:

1. Unit cost reduction via day-to-day routines, processes and procedures. These usually 'fall out' of continuous operational improvements as discussed earlier.
2. Deliberate quality improvement activities, eg clearly defined projects which are targeted on specific problem/cost areas, such as:

   - reduce wasted stationery by i) 25 per cent in six months
     ii) 50 per cent in twelve months
     iii) 90 per cent in fourteen months
   - increase the productivity of the cutting room by 60 per cent over the next twelve months
   - in six months double the utilization of the desk top publishing facility and reduce our cash flow to the external printers by 30 per cent
   - re-schedule plant maintenance so that the maintenance crew's overtime is cut by 60 per cent whilst maintaining plant efficiency
   - reorganize central administration so that equipment hire charges are reduced by 15 per cent within six months without increasing staff costs by more than 3 per cent.

3. By involvement of the people in the business. Get managers to set the improvement targets collaboratively and then empower the team members to find the solutions.

4. Measuring a 'Want to' Culture instead of a 'Have to' Culture

Undeniably the development of a 'want to' culture is the most difficult aspect of TQM, and yet it also happens to be the critical factor for success or failure. This will be discussed in greater detail in Chapter 7.

When measuring cultural change it is important to involve people throughout the business. Useful techniques include:

 John Smith Service Engineer	Can Train Others	High Skill Level	Medium Skill Level	Low Skill Level
Activity A		√		
Activity B		√		
Activity C		√		
Activity D				√
Activity E	√			
Activity F	√		√	
Activity G		√		
Activity H				√
Activity I	√			
Activity J			√	

Figure 1.9 *Skills appraisal card*

- before and after attitude surveys
- management style questionnaires
- interviews
- group discussion.

These invariably give qualitative data which is useful. Another useful barometer of cultural change is fluctuations or changes in levels of:

- sickness
- absenteeism
- team performance levels
- number of ideas in the suggestion scheme
- number of people leaving
- number of people applying to join
- number of people requesting appraisals
- level of support for sports and social events etc, etc.

These give quantifiable data which will support or contradict any reference in the vision to 'treating our employees as valued and respected people'.

5. Measuring a Highly Skilled Workforce

The ultimate measure of skill is, 'Can the person do the job to the required standard?' This forms the basis of the measuring system. We continually find that the success achieved by most organizations is directly proportional to the effectiveness of the work teams in the organization. Team effectiveness increases with the flexibility of its members, ie their being highly skilled in more than one task or role. Successful organizations not only actively encourage training but are equally energetic about the skills appraisal system – see Figure 1.9.

Skills cards such as the one shown in Figure 1.9 can frequently be found on display in the workplace, ie factory floor, office, assembly area, reception, instead of in the personnel officer's filing cabinet. Such clarity of skills identification not only contributes to the well-being of the individual but also provides the organization with an excellent mechanism of ensuring that there are no activities or tasks for which there is insufficient skill cover or flexibility.

TRAINER'S TIP

There is an obvious link between skills profiles and job specification. Therefore work *with* and not *in spite of* the personnel function. With TQM a job specification is a dynamic description of a job which will change periodically.

We hope you can see from the brief explanation that measuring an organization's progress towards the vision is essential and that these measures should reflect every key factor or characteristic of that vision.

How Does a Business Achieve the Vision?

There are some specific key areas which must all be addressed with equal vigor. These are shown in Figure 1.10.

A separate chapter in this book has been dedicated to each of these sections:

- Training and retraining (Chapter 4)
- Business Improvement Process (Chapter 5)
- Projects (Chapter 6)
- Management style and cultural change (Chapter 7)
- Effective personal and organizational communications (Chapter 8)

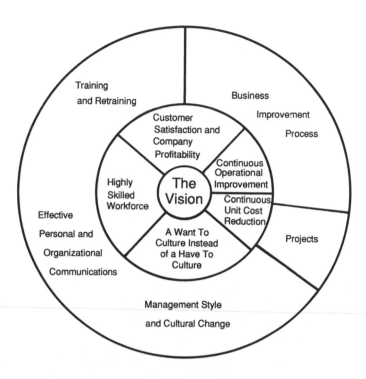

Figure 1.10 *Strategies for achieving the vision*

Consequently we shall give only a brief introduction here to each of these.

Training and Retraining

The achievement of any organization's commercial objectives is dependent more than anything else on the competence of the people employed. We will provide you with a thorough explanation (based on experience) of what is meant by training in a TQM organization and how it may differ from a more 'traditional approach'. We will look at policy, managing the learning experience, who is responsible, how to gain commitment, how to evaluate it.

Business Improvement Process

This primarily addresses the structure or systems approach to managing the organization. The aim is to build an internal supplier/customer chain which collectively is dedicated to giving the external customer what they want. In addition we will introduce a model called the 'cost of quality'. This enables teams, departments and organizations to break down costs item by item and consequently exercise more control over them. This will also highlight amongst other things which items take us closer to the vision and which ones take us further away from it.

Projects

Organizations are judged by customers, shareholders, employees and the general public, not only on how good the product or service is, but also on the way they manage and resolve (or not) their problems. How often have we heard about organizations which 'are going through a period of restructuring' and supporting noises such as 'it's about time they sorted themselves out', or 'I wish they'd make their mind up' or 'that's a difficult company to work with'.

Projects and project teams represent an approach to finding permanent solutions to problems instead of having to rely on 'quick fixes' or papering over the cracks. Project teams are usually created to address quality improvement problems, the resolution of which takes the organization closer to achieving the vision.

In this section you will be shown a number of tools and techniques such as project analysis, data collection, decision analysis, cause and effect diagrams etc. In addition the skills of working as a project team will also be dealt with.

Management Style and Cultural Change

TQM will not grow in an environment of autocracy, 'them and us', suspicion, where employees feel threatened or when the only opportunity they have to speak to their managers is when they've done something wrong! To build and sustain a TQM culture will require many managers and employees to behave differently, the lead of course coming from the manager. Issues of attitude, style and behaviour are high on the agenda for TQM.

The success of TQM also relies on building and maintaining effective relationships not only between the internal suppliers/customers, bosses and followers but also with external suppliers and customers.

Effective Personal and Organizational Communication

With TQM the need to communicate effectively exists like it has never existed before! With a traditional managerial style the emphasis has been on transmitting skills. These are still important but the TQM manager needs skills which are more to do with empowering people and fostering creativity. In addition various communication mechanisms will be looked at including team briefings, newsletters, notice boards and progress charts. With TQM the very nature of communication changes, from simply transferring information to a collaborative, problem-solving, esteem-building process which underpins quality relationships in the workplace.

TQM – A Concept?

'In my end is my beginning' T S Eliot

Total Quality Management is a demanding, disciplined yet humane way of managing an organization. It is more than a philosophy; it is:

- based on a set of solid principles and directives such as, 'Quality is determined by the Customer' and, 'we need to manage quality in as opposed to inspect error out';
- commercially very sound. It embraces critical issues such as financial performance and customer satisfaction;
- built on a framework of customer-centred systems and the internal supplier/customer chain. It is also equally passionate about establishing and monitoring standards of performance and conformance to specifications by using a variety of quality assurance techniques;
- an approach where continuous improvement becomes a way of life; and
- an approach which will succeed or fail depending on whether the organization's employees are 'with you' or 'agin you'.

TQM is more likely to succeed where there is obvious, visible top-down commitment to it and that means from the managing director. TQM has to be management led (see Figure 1.11). It requires not only involvement at the most senior level but also management participation in training events, their role-modelling desired characteristics, and also their questioning of all behaviours and activities which do not 'take us closer to the vision'. By behaving in this manner, senior managers will immediately start to impact on the culture of the organization.

How do we get the senior managers committed to TQM? This is a question frequently asked at the 'front end' of any TQM drive. The language shared by most senior managers is that of finance or, 'How this

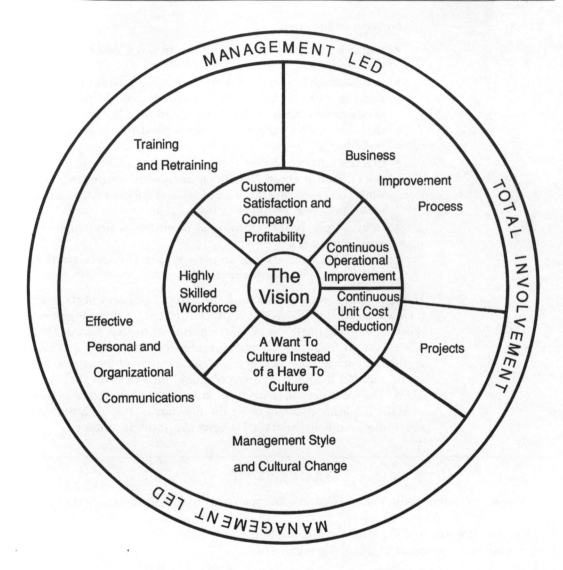

Figure 1.11 *The Model of Total Quality Management*

will affect the bottom line?' This therefore is the language you must use when operating at this level. You will probably find that not to do so will only end up with your either being shown the door (politely we hope), or being pushed into a negotiating position to which your only successful reply will be that of relating to 'the bottom line performance'.

Managers understand:

- that it is five times more expensive to win a new customer than keep an existing one;
- that what gives you a reasonable margin has more to do with keeping your cost base under control than bumping your prices up (because customers are funny about price!);
- that shareholders are looking for a good return on capital employed;
- that not only does it cost at least twice as much to visit a customer twice, when it could have been dealt with in one visit, but also while you're making the second call you are not making a first call somewhere else, resulting in lost income;
- what a 1 per cent improvement in efficiency per employee per annum means;
- that a labour turnover of 15 per cent per annum has a dramatic effect on cost and performance.

Managers will also be able to work out what 25 per cent of their annual turnover is. What they may not appreciate is that for many organizations the cost of poor quality is at least equivalent to that figure. (We will discuss this at length in Chapter 5 under 'cost of quality'.) It is using arguments such as these that gets the commitment of managers, starting at the top. Yet it would be unprofessional only to extol the virtues of TQM. The chief executive needs to know in as much detail as possible what the implications are of going on this journey. It is likely that she/he will want you to help them see far beyond just the advantages.

TRAINER'S TIP

As part of your introduction to TQM, ask your managers to list what they see as being:

a) the advantages of TQM for the organization;
b) the implications of TQM for the organization.

You may find it useful to compare this with our list below.

Advantages and Implications of TQM

These are just some general statements based on feedback from a similar exercise carried out in a major UK service organization.

Advantages of TQM for my organization	Implications of TQM for my organization
• Profitability ⎫ by satisfying • Job security ⎬ customers • Keep our costs down • Develop innovative approaches • Being the best • People enjoy working here • Good future • Everyone is accountable • Get to learn new things • My ideas get listened to and some get put into practice • I'm not just a number • Capital for re-investment • Quality organization	• Invest in training generally but particularly in TQM training • Managers to spend time involved in training • It could be difficult/confusing • It won't happen overnight • Up-front investment of both money and time in training and TQM awareness • If you can't change the people change the people • Managers have to get close to their people – the people might not like it • Everyone is going to be held accountable

With the managing director and senior management committed, the TQM journey can start (see Figure 1.12)

To achieve total involvement, and that means everyone in the organization being part of the TQM initiative, it would be helpful to look at it from an employee's point of view. The introduction of change is usually accompanied by feelings of anxiety, discomfort, fear and trepidation, and uncertainty. If we try to push in TQM too quickly it is likely that it will prove to be a difficult and painful process with a lot of casualties. With TQM, we need to create an expectation of change, to get people to regard change as something new, exciting, interesting and beneficial, something that will be looked forward to rather than something to be feared. It is unlikely that a half-hour presentation from the chief executive will do this, it is more likely that this attitudinal shift or desired state of mind will be achieved through a more measured approach, through gradual involvement, through periodically demonstrating the successes and rewards that have been achieved up to that moment in time. One thing is for sure, the sooner the organization adopts effective two-way communication and not only enters into a dialogue about what TQM is , but also listens to the expectations, fears, reservations, concerns and aspirations of their employees and realizes how TQM is compatible with meeting those expectations and eliminating those fears, the sooner TQM will be achieved. *TQM is about evolution not revolution.*

THE MODEL OF TOTAL QUALITY MANAGEMENT THE JOURNEY

Figure 1.12 *The model of TQM – the journey*

QUESTIONS FOR THE TQM TRAINER

In addition to the questions already presented you may find the following of some assistance when working with your customers.

- **About TQM**
  What do you think TQM is?
  What have your heard about TQM?
  What do you want to know about it?
  What TQM organizations do you know of?
  What do you think about those organizations?

What characterizes those organizations?
How do you think TQM differs from our current approach?

- **TQM and the Individual**
  How do you see this affecting you?
  How do you feel about it?
  What do you see as being the main features as far as your current role is concerned?
  Who is your customer?
  What support do you want from me?

- **About the main board and TQM**
  What does the main board think of this?
  How do you think they will respond?
  Why is that important to you?
  How do you feel about the board?
  What are you going to do to find out?
  What would you like me to do?

- **TQM and management teams**
  How will this affect the way you work together?
  How will this influence the way you work with your team?
  What do you think we should do?
  How do you feel about it?
  What goals should we set ourselves?
  Where are we going?
  What is our vision?
  How do we measure ourselves?
  How do our customers measure us?

- **TQM and customers**
  Who are our customers?
  What do our customers want from us?
  How do we know that?
  What do our customers think of us?
  How do our customers feel about us?
  How do we know?
  What effect will TQM have on the organization's customers?
  What effect will TQM have on your department's customers?
  What effect will TQM have on your customers?
  When was the last time you spoke to your customers?
  How frequently do you see your customers and who initiates this?

2 The Trainer and TQM

> SUMMARY <

- TQM training involves:
  knowing about TQM; helping clarify the vision; spreading the word; working alongside managers; acting as a training resource; working as an internal consultant.
- Helping techniques include:
  active listening; diagnostic questioning; confronting; giving advice.
- A TQM training consultant:
  establishes contact with the customer and forges a working relationship; agrees a contract; helps the customer gather data; helps the customer make sense of the data; helps the customer generate options, make decisions and plan; helps the customer implement the plan; finally arranges any necessary follow-up and disengages.
- Discovering what customers really need is central to TQM.
- Success is measured by your customer. Factors which help include:
  measurable objectives, measured back on the job; delivered right first time, on time, with change that sticks; actions which move towards the vision; actions which contribute towards profitability; keep checking with the customer now and in the future.

What is my Role in TQM?

Adopting TQM is likely to affect every facet of organizational life. This will include changes in:

- organizational structure;
- methods used to monitor activities;

- skills which people use;
- everyday behaviour of both staff and management.

Inevitably it follows that the trainer's role will also change. Instead of being employed as someone who simply designs and runs training courses you will become more concerned with facilitating learning and helping individuals and departments initiate, implement and come to terms with all of this change. We are convinced that competent TQM trainers will be essential if an organization is to adopt TQM successfully.

One way of examining the role of the TQM trainer is to contrast it with your role now. The following exercise may help:

EXERCISE: MY ROLE AS A TRAINER

Each of the following scales represents different views or training activities. Look at each in turn and give yourself a rating to indicate your approach to your work. Do try to be honest (if you wish you could also try getting the views of a few of your colleagues in training):

| 1 | 2 | 3 | 4 | 5 | 6 | 7 |

I have easy access to senior management and can influence their thinking. _____ I rarely (if ever) gain access to senior management.

Staff training is a managerial responsibility. _____ Staff training is the responsibility of the training department.

My role is mainly about helping my customers solve their own problems. _____ My role is mainly about designing training solutions to solve problems.

I design and develop unique development packages to meet my customer's needs. _____ I generally use standard training packages and 'fine tune' them to meet trainee needs.

	1	2	3	4	5	6	7

I have a high profile and am seen to work alongside managers in delivering training. ———————————— I generally deliver training alone or with other trainers.

I help and encourage managers to develop skills to train their own staff. ———————————— Training is a specialist job and I discourage managers from doing it themselves.

I directly help my customers address behavioural and relationship difficulties as and when they arise. ———————————— Behavioural and relationship difficulties are best tackled through a training course.

A significant proportion of my time is spent as an internal consultant. ———————————— My time is largely occupied with direct training activities.

I see everyone in the organization as my potential customer. ———————————— My customers are the people who attend my training courses.

My role involves helping customers think through their problems and design appropriate solutions. ———————————— My role involves designing training courses to solve organizational or departmental problems.

Once you have completed all of the scales have a look at the resulting profile. The nearer your crosses are towards the left-hand end of each scale, the closer you are to the activities and thinking required for TQM training.

This exercise should give you an overview of what you do now together with highlighting where you need to develop in order to move towards a TQM role. You may find it worthwhile to reflect on your profile and develop an appropriate personal action plan which takes you towards the actions described in the left hand column of the exercise.

TRAINER'S TIPS

All of the changes which your organization will need to embrace to implement TQM will benefit from the expertise of a skilled trainer – *but* it is up to you to get in and demonstrate this!

You have a great deal to offer a TQM initiative. Start attending to your own development needs now – if you don't they are likely to embark on TQM without you.

Remember, TQM is *their* initiative. Your role is to help as they work on understanding and implementing the inevitable and ongoing changes which TQM demands – *you cannot do it for them.*

What Skills will I Need?

All TQM training activities involve three core skills:

- skills in being an internal consultant;
- skills in training managers in training skills;
- skills in facilitating learning events.

The skills required to train managers in training skills and facilitate learning events (as opposed to running training courses) are probably closer to traditional training activities and will be picked up in later chapters. Here we will concentrate on the skills involved in becoming an effective internal consultant.

Being an internal consultant will involve you in influencing and advising all departments and levels of management (with little formal authority) to help them identify and implement TQM strategies. To be effective, your own efforts will have to be consistent with Total Quality thinking. That is, you will need to walk your talk – it is no good asking them to behave in a customer-centred way if you are not seen to do the same towards them.

Note. Throughout this chapter do bear in mind that when we refer to customers we mean anyone who seeks your help. This includes a manager who asks you to work with him/her on a problem in their department or someone who attends one of your training events.

Being a customer-centred training consultant means:

- starting where your customer is, not where you think he or she is;
- helping your customer decide what data or information they need to collect;
- helping your customer make sense of their data rather than doing it yourself;
- allowing your customer to diagnose which problems to tackle;
- where appropriate providing theory to help them make sense of the data or make decisions about courses of action;
- helping the customer gain commitment to the plan of action;
- assisting the customer to implement their decisions and arranging follow-up if appropriate;
- disengaging responsibly as soon as possible;
- ensuring the customer retains ownership of the problem and doesn't become dependent on you.

Although in outline very simple, the concepts and ideas underlying consulting are so crucial in TQM that we will spend some time examining them further. As a first step think about why organizations employ consultants and what they expect them to do.

In our experience consultants are usually engaged (either internally as members of staff, or as external consultants on a contract basis) in order to:

1. Help overcome difficulties, solve problems or implement change – hence the trainer is in effect a training consultant who uses training initiatives as the prime means of helping.
2. Provide help – this usually means offering advice, recommendations or solutions for organizational problems. But helping in this way can create enormous problems. Can you think why?

- Giving advice risks creating dependency on the part of the recipient. If similar problems arise in the future they will have to call on the consultant again for help. You might argue that this is a good way to ensure further business. But it does not foster a healthy relationship; the more that customers become dependent, the more they are likely to resent the inequality of the relationship.
- The recipient might not be sufficiently competent to implement the advice and have no other alternative other than to reject it.

- In situations where the advice is cascaded down through the customer's department, the advice may be modified, watered down, or at worst ignored.
- In situations where the advice is perceived as unacceptable, the consultant risks being rejected.

Perhaps you have identified other difficulties with giving advice, if so all well and good; our list is not meant to be exhaustive. Rather we hope it will serve as a note of caution. However, it would be wrong to conclude that giving advice never works. As a helping method it can be highly successful, but usually in cases where the recipient hasn't a clue what to do or is desperate for a solution.

As a final point it is worth noting that TQM consulting is about listening to customers (both internal and external), taking heed of what they want and what they have to say. Although giving advice may be appropriate at times it is used much less frequently than in other forms of consulting. So, if you can only give advice infrequently then what can you do for the rest of the time?

Earlier in this section we mentioned that it is important that the customer retains ownership of the problem. It follows therefore that whatever helping techniques we use must satisfy this requirement. With this in mind we would like to highlight three particular skills which can be very powerful when used appropriately.

1. Active Listening

Active listening may appear very passive, yet in practice it is a highly sophisticated helping technique. It means setting aside your own view of a problem and instead trying to understand it from the customer's point of view. Doing this can help the customer clarify their thinking and gain new insights into the problem. This will often allow them to find their own solution and plan of action. Obviously, in adopting this approach it is assumed that the customer has sufficient resources to find their own solution, but in our experience both managers and staff who are implementing TQM generally know what to tackle to improve quality. What they need is an opportunity to talk through their ideas; the training consultant is in an ideal position to provide this.

However, to use active listening effectively you need to be clear what it involves. A brief checklist of essential behaviours used in active listening is given below. As you will see it involves much more than simply behaving like a 'nodding donkey':

- open body posture;
- eye-contact;
- smiling, nodding, using expressions like 'uh-huh' to affirm your interest in what the customer says;
- confirming your understanding by paraphrasing or summarizing the customer's description of their situation;
- encouraging the customer to say more with expressions like 'tell me more';
- using silence to allow the customer time to think;
- avoiding any value judgements about what the customer is saying.

Active listening is invaluable when customers need help to think through a problem for themselves. In particular, it can be essential when they are paralysed from taking appropriate action because of unresolved feelings about a situation. For example, a colleague of ours was invited to help one department in an organization because of ongoing complaints by the staff about perceived deficiencies in a newly installed computer system that was designed to speed up order processing. After agreeing with the manager what was wanted she realized she would need to talk with the staff in the department to find out more about the problem. However, it was immediately apparent that they were so angry towards both management and the new system (which was imposed on them) that it was impossible to talk rationally about problems with the system. They were completely disabled by their anger. In response the consultant used active listening to acknowledge and work through how the staff felt. It slowly emerged that there was nothing actually wrong with the system but the staff were unsure how to use it. Their lack of knowledge was masked by anger and resentment at having the system foisted on them when, in their view, the old system was perfectly sound. For the consultant further work with the staff was easy; it consisted of using yet more active listening to help the staff work through and come to terms with their feelings. Their lack of knowledge about the system was then soon corrected using more traditional training techniques. To complete the work the consultant needed to give the manager feedback about how the system had been introduced and the effect it had created. This required a different helping technique which will be covered later.

2. Diagnostic Questioning

Sometimes active listening alone is insufficient to help a customer with their problem and on occasions a more focused technique can be helpful. Diagnostic questioning, as its name implies, uses open questions or statements to help the customer explore their problem more thoroughly.

This can highlight where there are significant gaps in the information available and as a consequence focus the customer on what information they need to collect to solve the problem. For example, in one of our TQM assignments we were working with six senior managers to help them develop as a team and clarify their purpose. As the work progressed it became apparent that each of them was working to a different agenda. To make progress we invited them to write down individually what they saw as the main purpose for the group's existence. As we expected (but to their surprise) we received six very different responses and the group had to engage in a considerable amount of further work to agree their common purpose. Prior to our simple question, 'what do you believe is the purpose of this team?', they had all assumed they were working towards a common goal. A simple diagnostic question illustrated that they were all pulling in different directions. Sometimes, however, rather than having a lack of information about the problem, the customer may be overwhelmed with information. In these instances diagnostic questioning coupled with an appropriate data analysis or presentation method can help them sort the wood from the trees. During TQM, one of your roles involves helping the customer find ways of analysing, recording and presenting information about quality. Techniques which can be used include:

- decision trees;
- force field analysis;
- critical path method;
- cost–benefit analysis;
- flow charts and algorithms;
- bar charts and histograms.

All of these techniques are ways of presenting or analysing otherwise complex information so that sensible questions can be posed to improve the process (some will be explained in more detail in later chapters). Here it is simply important to recognize that they fit hand-in-glove with diagnostic questioning.

In summary, diagnostic questioning consists of either asking open questions such as:

Who?
What?
Why?
Where?
When?
How?

or using these types of questions in conjunction with data analysis or presentation techniques to help the customer come to a decision.

3. Confronting

Confronting can be useful for TQM consultants when the customer is part of the problem and there are discrepancies between what they say they need to do (or are committed to in TQM) and what they actually do in practice. Confrontation highlights the mismatch between their thoughts, beliefs or values and actual behaviour.

These types of discrepancies are common in many organizations. For example, managers and staff may say they believe in quality yet continually overlook late deliveries, shoddy goods and poor service. Furthermore, rather than addressing the discrepancies, they make excuses to rationalize the mistakes and continue in the same self-defeating way. An illustration of this happened to one of the authors whilst writing this very section. He took a punctured tyre to a local garage for repair. The tyre was left late on a Saturday afternoon, to be collected on the following Monday. As it happened he could not retrieve the tyre on the Monday but called for it on the Tuesday instead. Despite the fact that the garage advertised that 'Customer Satisfaction Is Our Priority', the tyre was not ready. Instead he was offered the excuse that the garage could not get round to it as they had too much work on. Rather than confront the discrepancy with the sales assistant (who probably could do little about it anyway), the author took the tyre elsewhere. This time he chose a garage which did not advertise 'Customer Satisfaction' and had the job done immediately.

Actually carrying out a confrontation will involve the trainer in either:

- pointing out the discrepancy between what the individual (or group) says and what they do; or
- pointing out the implications/consequences if the individual or group continue with their current behaviour.

This illustration has its parallels in virtually every organization, sometimes with external customers and sometimes with internal. But what about your organization? Think about those parts of your organization which are your suppliers (ie, where you are the customer) and identify where there are discrepancies between what they say and do. When you have finished try repeating the exercise for those departments where you are the supplier (and therefore they are your customers). Do you have any insight into where there are discrepancies between what *you* say and do? If there are you would be well advised to do something to resolve the difference.

An important point to note about these discrepancies is that they rarely happen deliberately or as a result of malice. As human beings we just seem to have a capacity for saying and believing one thing yet acting in a manner contrary to that belief. For example, if you are in a partnership with someone, or have a spouse, no doubt you believe yourself to be a good partner. However, we would be prepared to wager that your partner will be aware of some discrepancies where your actions do not live up to your words. We only become aware of these when they are pointed out. This 'pointing out' is the substance of confrontation.

In Chapter 1 we mentioned that one particular role of the TQM trainer is acting as the conscience of the organization. This means recognizing and pointing out discrepancies between what is said about TQM and what is done – inevitably this involves confrontation.

The big danger with confrontation is that, if handled incorrectly, it may degenerate into conflict. Confrontation simply highlights discrepancies. It is not about scoring points, making value judgements, getting one up on the customer, winning, or teaching them a lesson – this is conflict and it can generate antagonism and hostility.

As an illustration of confrontation we would like to refer back to the example introduced in active listening where the consultant was called in because of complaints about the new computer system. You may recall that after using active listening the consultant was able to make progress with the staff group but was left to give the manager feedback about how the system was installed; this required confrontation. The consultant arranged a private interview with the manager where they discussed the manager's perception of how the system was introduced. He was of the opinion that it had been introduced in an open and democratic way where everyone had the opportunity to have their say. Very tactfully the consultant confronted him with the data she had collected from the staff. Initially he was astonished at this news but this soon gave way to anger. However, by holding to the substance of the confrontation and using active listening to deal with the manager's feelings, eventually they were able to use the experience developmentally as a lesson for the future.

This illustration also highlights that confrontation usually generates an emotional response. As a consequence you will probably need to follow it with active listening to deal with the emotion generated. This does not mean denying the content of the confrontation, it is simply the best way of dealing with the feelings which result. In saying this we recognize that confrontation can be a risky way of helping – particularly if the customer happens to be a senior manager. Nevertheless, confrontation is a valid way of helping, but it does need to be used with care.

TRAINER'S TIPS

Active listening can be an invaluable helping technique. Use it frequently – you might be surprised at the results.

Before confronting anyone – check your motives. If you are out to score points or show them they are wrong then you had better forget it!

We have looked briefly at three fundamental skills for the TQM training consultant – active listening, diagnostic questioning and confrontation. On occasions the fourth more common skill, giving advice, can be valuable but usually only when the customer hasn't a clue what to do or is desperate for a solution. Each of these skills could be the subject of a book in their own right and the discussion here has been very limited. However, for the present we hope you have sufficient detail to move on.

How is this Different from What I do Now?

Most trainers have some facility with the skills discussed in the previous section. So why all the fuss? TQM training is different in the way the skills are put together and to be effective you will probably find it helpful to have an understanding of a general model of the consulting process. A simple model* we use has seven broad phases:

1. Getting started – making contact with the customer (or re-establishing contact) and building a working relationship.
2. Contracting – finding out what the customer wants.
3. Collecting data – finding out what happens now.
4. Making sense of the data and problem diagnosis.
5. Generating options, making decisions and planning future action.
6. Implementing the plan.
7. Disengaging and arranging any necessary follow-up.

These phases are shown diagrammatically in Figure 2.1:

1. Getting Started

Starting a TQM consultation means establishing contact with the customer or, if you have worked with them before, re-establishing contact

*Adapted from Cockman, P, Evans, B, Reynolds, P (1992) *Client-centred Consulting: A Practical Guide for Internal Advisers and Trainers*, McGraw-Hill.

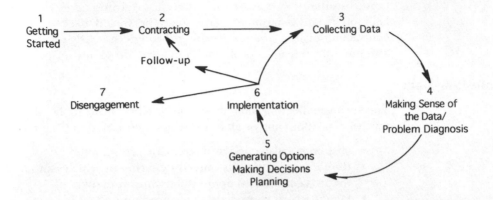

Figure 2.1 *The consulting cycle*

and starting to build a working relationship which is based on mutual trust and respect. To do this you will need to find out about the customer, the situation in their department and the particular issue(s) they wish to tackle. However, if the relationship is to be built on *trust and mutual respect* then the customer will also need to find out a few things about you and your department.

2. Contracting

Contracting is about discussing and making explicit both your own and the customer's expectations of the relationship:

- what the customer wants;
- what you are prepared to do;
- what the customer needs to do;
- how you will work;
- what boundaries exist.

Contracting is therefore about ownership and it is important that you make sure that the customer understands that you are not prepared to accept responsibility for the problem yourself. The responsibility for implementing TQM *must* remain with the customer – as we said earlier, you *cannot* do it for them.

You may be tempted to hurry through these first two phases, after all, it may be quite likely that you and your customers will know one another. If this is the case then beware: TQM initiatives are different – getting started on the right foot and thorough contracting are essential. Indeed

51

most consultants (whatever their specialism) would agree that problems later on in an assignment can usually be traced back to inadequate contracting or lack of trust. Rushing through the early stages of a TQM assignment can lead to problems later – you do so at your peril.

3. Collecting Data

This means collecting data about the situation now. In TQM this could involve data about any or all of the areas mentioned in Chapter 1:

- customer satisfaction and company profitability;
- the factors in the customer's department which can contribute towards continuous operational improvements;
- factors which contribute to reduced unit costs;
- the culture of the department or organization;
- the levels of skill in the customer's department;
- communication problems/barriers.

Obviously, exactly what data you collect will vary from one customer to another; indeed, if you are starting down the TQM road for the first time you will probably have to work with the customer to select which issue to tackle first. Remember your role is not collecting the data for the customer. It is to help the customer understand the need to collect data and install appropriate monitoring mechanisms to collect data in the future. TQM is not a once and only fad, it is an ongoing process which must continue beyond the point when you have disengaged.

4. Making Sense of the Data and Problem Diagnosis

Having collected the data the next step is to help the customer reflect, question and discuss the data in order to make sense of them in terms of the particular aspects of TQM they have chosen to tackle. That is, it is the customer's responsibility to diagnose where there are quality problems or changes which could be made to improve quality. In some cases the customer may find they have collected insufficient data and you may have to go back to the previous stage to collect more. In other cases the customer may be overwhelmed with data and you could find yourself helping to sort and present the data in a more understandable way before any diagnosis can be made. It may be possible to use some form of data analysis or presentation model to help the customer (as discussed in the previous section – see diagnostic questioning). In yet other cases you may be able to help by designing a questionnaire to elicit data. Whatever method you choose it is usually the customer who decides what data to collect and diagnoses what to do as a result. As a consultant this may present you with a significant dilemma. On the one hand you would wish to stay with the customer's diagnosis so that you remain customer-centred and do not take ownership of the problem. But you may discover that the customer wishes to tackle symptoms rather than an underlying problem. For example a customer may diagnose that high levels of absence which go without punishment are contributing to high costs. However, in your view high absence may be a result of the manager's own behaviour. As a consequence, if the manager is your customer, you may need to confront him/her with what you see as the implications of the diagnosis – not an easy task!

5. Generating Options, Making Decisions and Planning

Once the customer is clear on their diagnosis you should be in a position to help them generate as many options or potential solutions as possible. Sometimes you may be able to see more options than they can. At this point you must take care about introducing your ideas. Your customer may seize on one of them without really thinking it through and then blame you if it goes wrong. Therefore, in many situations it may be better to stick with the customer's chosen option even though you can think of a better one. Instead, your job is to challenge and confront so that the customer doesn't just take the easy option.

You might also have to help the customer think through the implications of their decision so that there is as little doubt as possible that the right decision has been made. Next you may need to help them formulate a plan of action. Without a clear plan very little is likely to happen. However, your job is to encourage the customer to question the plan, anticipate what could go wrong and ensure that adequate resources are set aside (including time and money). Finally you might be involved in helping the customer get commitment from others in their department before implementation.

6. Implementing the Plan

It is often tempting to leave customers prior to implementation and assume that action plans will be turned into action. As a TQM training consultant you cannot afford to do this. The only way that you can be sure that the plan is implemented is to be there while it happens. However, it is important to make sure you *do not* take a leading role. This is your customer's show, not yours. Your job is to monitor, mentor, encourage, support, when necessary confront and at times counsel – not take ownership. Remember, if the problem belongs to the customer, so does the solution.

53

7. Disengaging and Arranging Follow-up

The final step in customer-centred consulting is disengagement and, where necessary, arranging follow-up. Once the plan has been implemented and you are sure your customer knows how to continue unaided it is time to leave and move on to a different TQM assignment (perhaps in another department). You will need to stay around to make sure the new way of working leads to progressive improvements in quality, but in this assignment you should by now be largely redundant. It is important to remember not to stay with the customer too long as they are likely to begin to resent your presence. This is a difficult decision. In some ways it is a bit like the dilemma a pilot must face when deciding whether to give a trainee permission to fly solo. You want to make sure they don't crash, but at the same time you must let go sometime and the longer you stay the more they will feel you don't trust them. There are no easy answers. As an internal consultant this might be less of a problem as you are unlikely to be leaving the customer forever. You may bump into them in the organization and, if you have done a good job, no doubt you will be invited back at some point to help them take new steps towards further quality improvements.

Having completed the model of TQM consulting it is now probably appropriate to review how far your approach to training is consistent with the model presented here. If your approach is broadly similar then you are likely to experience fewer difficulties in taking on a TQM role. If, on the other hand, your actions are vastly different you may have to do a major rethink – TQM training could prove quite a challenge.

How Can I Start?

Exactly where you start depends on where you are now. Satisfactory starting points could include:

- ensuring you know what TQM is about and thinking through the implications for your organization;
- reviewing how you conduct training currently and identifying how your role will change to become more consistent with TQM;
- reviewing the skills you need to develop to carry out this new role. You might think about each of the seven phases in the TQM consulting model and identify any skill deficiencies;
- finding out as much as you can about your company – not only what is produced but also how it is doing financially and any other indicators you can dig out (the reason for this will become clear later).

Most important of all, if your company has not yet started on TQM, read the rest of this book and start talking about it. Above all – start right now!

Who are my Customers?

Throughout this chapter we have kept on referring to your customers rather than clients or trainees or any other name you may use to describe the people or departments you try to help. This way of thinking is fundamental to TQM. Starting to think in terms of customers changes the whole nature of the relationships we create. However, rather than thinking about customers in an abstract sense, perhaps it is time to get down to sorting out who are your actual customers by working through the exercise on page 56.

We call this a supplier/customer chain because all of your customers in turn have their suppliers and customers. As a consequence, in TQM the whole organization chart could be drawn in terms of a sequence of interlocking supplier/customer chains. For a TQM organization this would actually make more sense than the more formal organization chart. We will examine these chains in much greater detail later when we look at the business improvement process. However, as a preliminary we can prepare for this by looking at your bit in the chain right now.

Although your suppliers are important and not to be forgotten, for the moment we will concentrate on the customer side of your diagram. To make sure you have completed this as fully as possible the following prompts might help:

- Look back over your training plan and identify all of the departments you have worked with, and then ask:
  - which are regular customers?
  - have any been 'one-off' customers who used you once but never again?
  - if so, why?
- Look back through your diary for the last year or so:
  - what meetings did you attend with potential customers?
  - did these meetings elicit any actual training work?
  - if not, why?
- Are there any departments where you have never worked, but feel you could usefully make a contribution to their efforts?
  - if so, how can you arrange to talk with them?
- Are you aware of any departments who use external training agencies without consulting you, where you could do the work just as adequately?

– if so, why might this be?

When you have identified all of your customers your next step is to make sure you know what they want.

EXERCISE: MY CUSTOMER/SUPPLIER CHAIN

Spend a few minutes completing the following diagram to clarify your customer/supplier relationships at work. Start by filling in your name in the space provided above 'TQM Trainer'. Then complete the 'suppliers' side of your equation by answering the following question – 'Who in my organization provides me with a service?'.

Once this side is complete move to the other side and list all of the people or departments who you supply with a service, ie, 'Who are my customers?'

SUPPLIERS   CUSTOMERS

?   . . . .   ?

TQM TRAINER

You may need to keep coming back to this diagram. If you have never thought of your relationships (both inside and outside of the organization) in terms of customer or supplier this may take some time to become familiar. As a consequence you may find that new names keep popping up in your mind as time goes by.

How do I Know What my Customers Want?

Along with company profitability, knowing what your customers want is a central pillar of TQM. How do you establish these needs at present in your company?

In most training departments, customers' needs are determined through discussion. Usually at the start of an assignment training needs are agreed and the actual training is then designed around these needs. In TQM training an important point is recognizing that the customer may need help to find out what they really need rather than what they think they need. Training can sometimes be used as an easy option. In TQM we highlight this as the distinction between real needs and felt needs. Perhaps a brief illustration will help to clarify this point.

Some months ago a colleague of ours who was employed as a training officer in a large company had just completed a long series of training courses to help the workforce improve the quality of their reinstatement work (ie, filling in and re-surfacing holes which have been dug in public highways to gain access to essential service pipes). This work had been initiated in the first place in response to complaints from the public (ie, external customers) about the state of road surfaces after they had been excavated. The problem started to emerge when the director concerned with this branch of the organization called in our colleague and told him that reinstatement costs were excessive. Furthermore, despite the training which had already been carried out, in the director's view the workforce did not know what they were doing and would require immediate re-training. Our colleague was astonished, he could not believe what he was being told. However, rather than accept the director's diagnosis of the problem he decided to investigate further. As a first step, he invited into the training centre a sample of the workforce and, without further training, asked them to carry out a reinstatement exercise. The results demonstrated that they knew exactly what to do and hence the problem was not one of skill deficiency or lack of knowledge.

Armed with these results he went back to confront the director. Effectively the confrontation consisted of agreeing with the director that reinstatement costs were high and therefore they could assume that the work was not being carried out adequately on the job, but pointing out that when tested in the training centre, the workforce knew exactly what to do. Therefore the problem was not one of lack of training and the root problem must lie elsewhere. Eventually the director accepted what our colleague was saying and agreed to further investigation. To carry out the investigation our colleague worked alongside managers and supervisors in the department and they quickly discovered that the real problem lay in inadequate availability of tools and equipment and poor scheduling for delivery of re-surfacing materials on site. In short, the men doing the work didn't have the correct tools or materials to do the job at the time they were needed – difficulties which were relatively simple to correct.

If our colleague had colluded with the director's diagnosis the organization would have spent a small fortune on unnecessary re-training. However, by collecting the evidence and 'sticking to his guns', he was able to help his customer root out the real problem (tools and materials) and thereby reduce reinstatement costs. As a by-product the reputation of training was enhanced no end.

For us this illustration highlights the need to work with customers to determine their real needs rather than simply accepting their felt needs at face value. In some cases this can be difficult as customers might not be able to express easily what they want. The illustration also highlights the need for the TQM trainer to act as a consultant, at times being prepared to confront senior members of the organization.

Here are a few other ideas for helping customers determine their needs:

- Wherever possible help customers to express their needs behaviourally; ie, 'What is it that you want *to do* differently?', and make sure they answer in terms of behaviour – this has implications for measuring success.
- Help the customer to question whether their needs take them closer to the vision or further away from it.
- Keep asking 'What are the implications for the bottom-line?', profitability is equally important.
- Above all, keep on digging. Your customers are your lifeblood – if you can't find out what they want you have no chance of implementing TQM.

How Much do I Need to Know about the Business?

Before we embark on any discussion, try to answer the following questions:

- What service/products does your company provide?
- How many people does your company employ?
- How is it structured?
- What are the important strategic business issues which the company must tackle over the next five years?
- What are the key financial indicators for your company?
- How well is it performing on these indicators?
- What are the key output/service level indicators for your company?
- How well is it performing on these indicators?

In our experience trainers are usually quite well informed about what the business does, less well informed on strategic issues, and poorly informed on financial indicators. Unfortunately at senior management levels it is the strategic, financial and business indicators which are important. It follows therefore that if you are to have any influence or credibility at this level you need to be able to talk in their language. The only way these groups are likely to become interested and committed to TQM and training is if they are expressed in terms which relate to company performance. Therefore, the sooner you start thinking about your work in terms of its effect on the bottom line, the better. The answer to the question 'How much do I need to know about the business?' is simple – a lot and in language which senior managers understand.

If terms like 'return on capital employed', 'gearing' etc, fill you with terror, fear not; we are not suggesting that you need to become an accountant. But you do need to be familiar with the language and what it means for your company. Clearly this is not the place to give you a crash course in interpreting financial information. Other authors have done this far more effectively than we could and you would be well advised to read a few as part of your personal development plan.

TRAINER'S TIPS

Start to find out as much as you can about how your company is performing. Reading and asking questions about the annual report and accounts for the last two or three years is a good place to start.

Arm yourself with as much knowledge about the business as you can – when you speak with senior management you must be able to talk in their language.

Thinking about training in terms of its effect on performance and profitability is also relevant for measuring success, as we will see next.

How do I Know if I'm Successful?

Measuring training success in TQM depends on knowing what the customer wants and how they measure success. This may be something of a departure from traditional practice; however we would argue that the way the trainer should measure success is in exactly the same way as the customer. This may mean abandoning old favourites such as end of course 'happy sheets' or man-training days, and instead accepting the customer's criteria (which will probably be linked to bottom-line performance measures).

However, if we can be sure we know what the customer really wants and our efforts help them meet their needs, then we should be on course for success. This is why it is important for a customer's needs to be expressed behaviourally. Behavioural needs are easily translated into behavioural training objectives and these are measurable. Training will then be about achieving these objectives – getting it right first time, on time and in such a way that the change sticks. Our checklist for achieving success includes the following:

- Where direct training is involved use measurable objectives, measured back on the job.
- Delivered right first time, on time and in a way that ensures that change sticks.
- Actions must help the customer move closer towards the vision.
- Actions must contribute to overall profitability.
- Finally, perhaps most important of all, keep checking with the customer to make sure their needs are being met now and continue to be met in the future.

QUESTIONS FOR THE TQM TRAINER

- Do you *really* help your customers solve their problems?
- Can you – listen actively?
    - question diagnostically?
    - confront when needed?
- What barriers exist to building trust and mutual respect with your current customers?
- Think about one of your current customers. What are their expectations of you? – what are your expectations of them? Have these been discussed?
- Who are your customers?
- Who are your suppliers?
- What additional knowledge do you need about the company you work for?

3 The Vision

SUMMARY

- The vision is the starting point for all TQM initiatives – it should state as clearly as possible exactly what the company is trying to achieve. It acts as a beacon guiding and illuminating decision-making and action.
- A quality vision statement will make explicit the organization's approach to:
    - customer satisfaction;
    - organizational performance;
    - product/service quality;
    - how employees will be treated;
    - social responsibility.
- Whilst the vision can be a powerful force for positive change, unless carefully monitored it can also have negative consequences.
- To be effective the vision should offer a goal which is always just out of reach but never that far out of reach that it is not worth striving towards.
- Without *full agreement and commitment* at the top, TQM will not work.
- Once the vision has been created it needs to be cascaded down to every single employee.

What is the Vision?

The vision, or mission statement as it is known in some companies, describes the goal which the organization is striving towards. It is the essential starting point for all TQM initiatives. The vision should make absolutely clear exactly what the organization is trying to achieve. As such it becomes a beacon for everyone in the organization illuminating and guiding all decision-making and action.

61

EXERCISE: THE VISION IN MY ORGANIZATION

Obtain a copy of the vision for your organization and read it very carefully, then on a separate sheet of paper try to answer the following questions:
   a. What does it say about customer satisfaction?
   b. What does it say about organizational performance?
   c. What does it say about product/service quality?
   d. What does it say about how employees will be treated?
   e. What does it say about social responsibility?

Being aware of, and the relative ease with which you obtained a copy of, the vision for your organization, are important indicators of whether the company is serious about quality. In TQM organizations the vision is known by everyone from the boardroom to the shopfloor. It is recognized and acknowledged that everyone contributes to quality no matter what their station.

The questions posed in the exercise were included to help you check out the breadth and clarity of the vision in your company. Each of the five areas mentioned are important components of a vision in TQM terms. How far the vision for your company can respond to those questions satisfactorily is another indicator of whether quality is taken seriously.

Superb examples of vision statements exist in many companies and it would be practically impossible to select one as being 'the best'. We have therefore constructed the following example combining the main features from a number of excellent sources.

Case example: Soft Sparkle Inc

Vision

We are a major international manufacturer of soft drinks. Our purpose is to develop our products consistently and continuously to meet the requirements of our customers. By focusing on this we will prosper, be profitable and help our customers to achieve the same.

Our Values

The manner in which we work towards our vision is as important as the vision itself. Our central values include:

Partnership

Partnerships with our customers and suppliers are critical for our success. The partnerships we create will be built on honesty and respect. We will actively collaborate with all our partners – by working in this manner we believe our actions will be mutually beneficial to both our partners and ourselves.

People
We are only as good as the people we employ. We will treat our people with dignity and respect – their skills are crucial for our success. Consequently, participation and involvement will be encouraged at all times and at all levels.

Products
Our products are a reflection of our people. We will strive for continual improvement in all our activities. Our products will be of the highest quality and will consistently satisfy our customers' needs.

Profits
As a company we are ultimately measured by our profitability. Profits are required for us to survive, grow, offer employment and prosper.

Our Priorities

Quality
Quality comes first – this is non-negotiable.

Customers
We exist to serve our customers. Everyone in our organization will understand that we are privileged to serve our customers. The vitality which we demonstrate in our relationships with customers is directly proportional to our success.

Suppliers
We will build and maintain long-term healthy relationships with our suppliers. Without this our future would be uncertain.

Continuous improvement from everyone
Continuous improvement will embrace every aspect of our work. Our employees will be encouraged to look for and find ways to contribute to our development. This will be acknowledged and rewarded.

Trusting and trustworthy
We will pursue our business in a trusting and trustworthy manner. This will extend to our people, our suppliers, our customers and the society of which we form a part. We are committed to equal opportunities and our doors are open to people from any race, sex, age or disability group.

If you come from an organization which does not have a vision of such breadth and scope then you may find it hard to accept that such vision statements exist in commercial companies. We can only assure you that they do – this example is based on reality.

63

Why is the Vision Important?

Perhaps the best rationale of why the vision is important is given by Anita Roddick of Body Shop:

'If you have an itsy bitsy vision, you have an itsy bitsy company'

Where a company does not have a guiding vision which is understood by all employees, then different sections of the company may pull in different directions. In the absence of any future goal, individual managers are likely to formulate their own ideas often leading to internal competition, 'them and us' attitudes, mistrust and low motivation. Staff may begin to perceive themselves as mere numbers on the payroll rather than valued for their contribution.

The last decade has seen an enormous growth in consumer pressure. There are now pressure groups in most areas of business life; we have seen the growth of TV programmes dedicated to seeking out and vilifying poor service and shoddy (or unsafe) goods. These pressure groups demand increasingly higher quality from all organizations whether they are publicly owned or private.

We believe the sensible response to customer pressure is through organizational transformation – that is, moving towards a type of organization which achieves quality through ownership, personal responsibility and the desire to do a good job. This is TQM. It starts with clarity of purpose – the vision – but the real job lies in living the message each day, every day, throughout the company. This book is devoted to helping you make that happen.

Are There any Dangers?

Having spent some time looking at the vision and why it is important, it would be wrong of us to continue without also questioning whether there are any dangers in adopting a visionary approach.

In our view the greatest danger in TQM lies in the nature of its power. Systems, organizations and leaders who are able to articulate a vision have the power to move people (or nations for that matter). Once wedded to some sense of purpose they can enthuse people to strive ever harder towards a distant vision. Gandhi, Martin Luther King and other great leaders all used visionary messages to change the course of history. Similar forces can be put to work in organizational settings. When an organization espouses and lives by lofty and noble ideals it has the capacity to unlock a tremendous amount of power in its members.

However, this power can also have the capacity to burn people out, take over their private lives and cause them to become ruthless and lacking in compassion for anyone who does not share their sense of purpose. Evidence for this is already beginning to appear in a few Japanese firms which, according to many reports, demand and get a great deal from their employees; unfortunately they also burn some of them out along the way

Whilst visionary forces can provide a very potent power for change, they can also unlock the 'daimonic' side of human beings. The psychologist Rollo May used the expression 'daimonic' to describe the dark side of man's nature which seeks expression and impact on the world without regard for cost or consequence. When held in check, the daimonic can provide individuals with the stimulus for great achievements or contributions. But when out of control it can burn them out. In TQM the possibility of tapping the daimonic in people is very real and needs to be constantly guarded against. The vision in TQM should provide the distant goal but not at the expense of a few within the organization becoming victims of their own enthusiasm.

TRAINER'S TIP

As a TQM trainer you can fulfil an invaluable role by keeping a 'weather eye' open for the emergence of the daimonic in staff and, if necessary, stepping in to help them redress the balance.

What Should the Vision Include?

As we saw in the example quoted earlier, vision statements which illustrate best practice generally address five concerns.

1. Customer Satisfaction

Achieving customer satisfaction continually and consistently is essential and therefore deserves to be included in the vision statement. But remember, whether your customers are internal or external, it is essential that you know what they want. If your customer information is flawed your chances of achieving customer satisfaction are remote.

2. Organizational Performance

The organization must remain profitable and there is no harm in making this explicit in the vision. However, in TQM, knowledge about financial indicators and how the organization is performing needs to be widely available. The more that employees are aware of, and able to see the linkage between what they do and how the company performs, the better.

3. Product/Service Quality

This is the cornerstone of TQM and no vision would be complete without it. In TQM quality is achieved through ownership and personal responsibility rather than giving the sole responsibility for quality to a specific quality control department. However, there are exceptions particularly where health and safety issues are crucial. But even in these cases quality assurance should be conceived as a partnership rather than a police force.

4. Treatment of Employees

Customer satisfaction, high quality and profitability can only be achieved through the cooperation of all employees. This will not happen if they work in systems which are oppressive or de-humanizing. If employees are to work with you, then it is best to state how they will be treated. This is fundamental and must be recognized within the vision.

5. Social Responsibility:

It is possible in the short term for an organization to achieve TQM with little concern for social responsibility. However, organizations do not exist in a vacuum, they take from wider society and, in our view, must in return act responsibly. In the longer term it is in their own best interest. The more that organizations are prepared to state this in their vision, the more they will gain in respect and support from wider society.

Is it a Journey or a Destination?

If you look back and re-read the vision statement illustrated earlier you will note that it is written in such a way that the goal is unattainable. Contrast it with the following fragment of a vision.

Handy-Tech Ltd

Mission

Handy-Tech is a rapidly growing manufacturer of power-driven hand tools. We intend to become the market leader in our section of the manufacturing market, whilst at the same time ensuring we always remain profitable.

In this case the goal is attainable. As a vision it may be adequate if Handy-Tech has a long way to go to become the market leader. But assuming it actually gets there, what then? Presumably the vision will have been realized and everyone can relax; what else is there to strive for? Unfortunately this is a recipe for complacency and in any area of business that spells disaster. Hence, you will find that companies which adopt best practice always describe their vision in such a way that it is unattainable.

Spelling out the vision in any organization looks easy but in fact is quite difficult to get right. On the one hand the vision needs to be unattainable, but at the same time it should not appear that far away that it leads to demoralization. Somehow a balance needs to be found that is just out of reach but not so far out of reach that it is not worth striving towards.

TRAINER'S TIP

As a TQM trainer you are probably ideally located to observe and give feedback on whether the vision for your organization catches this balance.

To return to the original question, 'Is TQM a journey or a destination?', unequivocally, the vision should set the goal for a never-ending journey.

Where does the Vision Come From? Who Should Produce it?

For TQM to be successful the vision has to be produced by the very top group within an organization. They will be the only group which is in a position to decide the core values the organization should adopt. TQM is not the kind of initiative which can be driven upwards from the bottom and any bottom-up approach is doomed to failure.

Having decided to adopt TQM, the very first action must be for the senior group to meet to hammer out and reach agreement on the vision for the company. This is not the kind of task which can be delegated to a working party and then given nodding assent or 'rubber stamped' by the top. This cannot be emphasized too strongly: the senior group needs to give its whole-hearted commitment to whatever vision it creates. *Without full commitment from the top TQM will not work.*

In many large companies commitment to the vision is often emphasized by appointing at executive level someone with specific overall responsibility for quality. This appointment may not be at the top level itself, but if not, it needs to be at a level which is sufficiently senior for the individual to have access to, and considerable influence with, the top.

Reaching agreement on the vision for a company may appear easy but in practice is often quite a challenge. In our own work with organizations where we have been engaged to help clarify a vision, we have frequently worked with senior groups which, at the outset, claimed to have a common understanding of what the business was about and where it was going. However, within minutes it has been evident that each member of the group interprets the so called 'common understanding' differently. Where this is the case (as it usually is) much detailed discussion and appreciation of the differing viewpoints has to be ploughed through before agreement is reached. If there is a lack of unanimity at the top there is no chance of TQM succeeding lower down.

Once the vision has been agreed at the top, what happens next?

What Happens Next?

Two sets of actions need to be carried out in fairly rapid succession. First, members of the top group need to work through the implications of the vision for their own behaviour as managers, and more importantly, start putting this into practice – both in their behaviour towards one another and in their contact with other staff. Second, the vision needs cascading down through all levels of the company to every single employee. In large organizations training is likely to be heavily involved at this stage (particularly if it is known for advocating TQM). This cascading involves much more than simply telling people. Cascading the message seeks to:

- start the process of getting the whole organization to *own* the vision;
- forewarn everyone that considerable change in every department will follow in the near future.

Ownership is about the degree to which people feel personally responsible for any change which affects them together with how committed they are towards taking any necessary action. To explore this further you might like to reflect on significant changes which have affected you in your working life. In particular think about changes you have felt negative about and the reasons why, and changes you have felt positive about and the reasons why.

In our experience, the factors which affect the way people feel about change can be placed into the following categories:

- how much information we have about the change;
- how far we participate in any decisions about change;
- how much we trust the initiator of the change;
- what kind of earlier experience we have had of any similar change;
- what impact any change is likely to have on our relationships with other people;
- our individual personality.

All of these factors will affect how people respond to change. Perhaps your reactions to change will fall into similar categories? For the TQM trainer the important point is that all of these factors must be taken into account. Some of them, such as previous experience of change, are in the past and there is little you can do to re-write history. However, with a little forethought on your part, you can influence the others. Hence, if you want employees to own the vision it seems pretty important that:

- they are informed;
- they are able to participate meaningfully in any decisions about change;
- trust is built up with the initiator of change;
- they are able to work through the implications of any change on their relationships with others.

All of these points will be brought out more fully in subsequent chapters when we discuss in detail the changes which departments may need to implement. For the present, we will turn to examine your role as the vision is being created.

What is My Role?

The exact nature of your role will depend on the stage at which you are brought into the TQM process. One possibility is where you are involved from the start – working with the senior group to create the vision. Whether you are an external consultant or an internal trainer the process for doing this is exactly the same. However, as an internal trainer your role could start when the vision is cascaded down to employees. A third variation could involve your working collaboratively with an external consultant. The rest of this section will look in detail at each of the these scenarios and suggest possible courses of action.

Where you are Able to Work Directly with the Senior Group

Perhaps the best way to approach this situation is as a consulting assignment. As such you will need to follow each of the phases in the consulting cycle:

Establishing contact; building a working relationship
You may already know the senior group quite well or be meeting them for the first time – either way you will need to build an open and honest relationship with them.

Contracting
Overlook this phase at your peril – both you and the group need to be absolutely clear what you expect from one another. Do not be seduced into rushing immediately into the task; also, remember your role in this assignment is to help them reach agreement – not to write the vision for them.

Collecting data
The data you will be helping the group collect are each individual's perception of what they believe the vision should be – it is important therefore that they all contribute, are heard and have their contributions acknowledged.

Making sense of the data
This involves discussion and understanding of each individual's view. Your role is to facilitate this discussion, ie, help them clarify and work through disagreements; confront inconsistencies and/or omissions. You might also need to help them make sense of the emerging vision in terms of their own behaviour towards one another – for example, if they say they want employees to be recognized and valued then it is important they recognize and value one another. This could involve you in confronting the here and now behaviour of the group.

Generating options; making decisions; planning
This involves helping the group look at its options for a vision and selecting the one which represents best practice for the organization – remember this must be a consensus decision; a majority vote will not do. Having done this the group may then need further help to plan how to carry the vision forward from here.

Implementation
This is likely to be about cascading the vision through the organization and obtaining ownership and commitment from everyone.

TRAINER'S TIP

When working with members of the senior group it is important to get them to think about the implications of what they are creating – it is likely to mean major changes for their own behaviour and style of management.

To help them check out the breadth of the emerging vision – get them to consider whether it contains all of the five elements which should be included in a vision.

Where an External Consultant is Invited to Work with the Senior Group

If the work of creating the vision is handed over to a consultant then as an internal trainer your role is one of supporting their efforts and paving the way for cascading TQM through the wider organization. In practice this means:

- Talking about TQM – to colleagues in training and other managers; talk about the ideas behind it; the advantages it has to convey; how TQM might work in your organization. The more that you become (and are seen to become) the advocate of TQM the better.
- Where others show interest, guiding them to other sources of information; eg, other relevant books on TQM; contacts in other organizations which operate TQM. In short, become the source of knowledge about TQM in your organization.
- Forging as many links/contacts as you can with other TQM organizations to broaden your own base of knowledge and (more importantly) make this known.

All these actions will help make you the obvious choice to take over when the consultant leaves.

Where your Involvement Consists of Working Collaboratively with an External Consultant

This has much in common with working directly with the senior group. No matter how far the TQM initiative has progressed by the time you become involved you will need to:

- Get to know the consultant(s) and build a sound working relationship with them.
- Explore one another's expectations of the relationship – how you can work together effectively; what you both (all) want to achieve in your work with customer groups; what skills each of you bring to the relationship; how you can support each other.

Once you have established a sound relationship then your work with customer groups will have to be carefully planned. If you are likely to be working together as the assignment progresses then all of the points mentioned in the last scenario will also be applicable.

TRAINER'S TIP

As an internal trainer, at first you may find it uncomfortable to work with 'outsiders'. Various issues may arise:

- Who is the expert?
- Who is in charge?
- Who makes the decisions?
- Background/cultural differences.

Issues like these may get in the way. It is important therefore that you raise them and discuss them thoroughly. Remember, you need to develop a partnership relationship!

Whatever your involvement in creating the vision, internal trainers are likely to be heavily involved with helping cascade the message down through the organization and, subsequently, working with individual departments to help them translate the vision into practical action. You will also need to work through the implications of the vision for training itself so that you are sure that you provide a quality training service. This is another area where you could do some useful preparation. Indeed you will probably find it worthwhile turning back to the illustration of the vision we described earlier and thinking through the implications of this for your work if you were employed in that company.

QUESTIONS FOR THE TQM TRAINER

- Beware – does the vision describe a goal which can be achieved?
- Does the vision include all five elements?
- Is the vision too far out of reach?
- Is the senior group committed, in both words and action?
- Will the vision be carried down through the whole organization?
- Has anyone been left out – cleaners, part time staff, staff who work on late shifts?

4 Training and Retraining

▷ SUMMARY ◁

- Training must be 'results oriented' and made to stick in the workplace – training is about change and improvement.
- Learning is a process that needs to be managed.
- Line managers are responsible for training and need to be involved from very early in the process.
- Learning agreements can be a very powerful way of keeping the learner focused on 'Why are we doing this?'
- Both the line manager and the trainer must support the learners re-entry to the workplace – the effective application of new skills in the workplace is directly proportional to the effort and energy the line manager puts in.
- On-the-job training is vitally important.
- Evaluation of training should use the customer's criteria based on business performance indicators.

What is the Training Process?

When carried out properly, training enables both people and organizations to create more opportunities and at the same time make more of any opportunities which arise – in TQM this is essential. Fundamentally the training process is about helping people to learn and by now you will have realized that TQM will involve learning at all levels. This will extend from the boardroom to the shopfloor – no one will be exempt. In the previous chapter we discussed the trainer's role in helping create the vision and in Chapter 1 we identified other specific key areas which must be addressed when implementing TQM; these were:

- The business improvement process.
- Projects.
- Managerial style and cultural change.
- Effective personal and organizational communications.

As you will see in subsequent chapters, tackling each of these areas will have enormous training implications. As a consequence, training is likely to take a much more prominent position within the organization. However, it is important to recognize from the outset that training is a managerial process rather than an event.

J A G Jones* outlined a simple three-stage model for describing the training process; it involves:

- Getting it right.
- Doing it well.
- Making it stick.

In our view the TQM training process involves a modification of these ideas; this is illustrated diagrammatically in Figure 4.1.

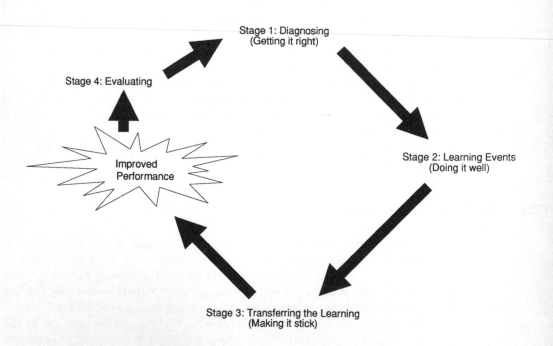

Figure 4.1 *Managing the TQM learning process*

*Jones, J A G (1985) 'Training and Intervention Strategies', *Training and Development*, February.

No matter which aspect of TQM you are addressing this model is fundamental for helping people learn. The rest of this chapter will be devoted to examining in detail each stage of this process.

How do I Diagnose Training Needs?

Diagnosing training needs is about carrying out a detailed analysis to ensure that any subsequent training or learning experience is focused and contributes to improved performance. Whether diagnosing needs for an individual, team, department or organization the principles are precisely the same in each case. From the start you need to be involved with the organization and in touch with whatever is going on. Whilst collecting data for the diagnosis you will have to work very closely with the management team.

TRAINER'S TIP

In a Total Quality organization the line manager is heavily involved and committed to the development of their team. This means they need to be competent at diagnosing team and individual needs. It follows therefore that your role includes developing this ability in managers.

Fundamentally diagnosing training needs is concerned with finding out whether people are doing their jobs properly. Therefore, before we go any further it would be useful to reflect on what this means to you. In our view, to do a job properly means that the individual job holder:

- knows what to do (specification);
- knows how to do it (skill and knowledge);
- is equipped to do it (resources);
- knows how well it needs to be done (measurement and comparison);
- is able to effect it (involvement);
- wants to do it (motivation).

In TQM these are all critical factors which need to be taken into account when asking questions in order to diagnose training needs. The quality and relevance of the analysis is usually in direct proportion to the quality and relevance of the questions either you (the trainer) or the line manager ask, as well as who you ask.

Listed below are a few questions which may prove helpful during the diagnostic phase. Some of the questions can be posed to both the manager and the people who are doing the job, others are designed for one or the other; the distinction should be evident from the question.

- Why are we doing this?
- What tasks cause difficulty?
- What objectives are met/not met?
- What will it look like when the problem no longer exists?
- What changes can be envisaged in the next year or so?
- What is likely to challenge the person in the near future?
- Are there going to be any changes in responsibilities or circumstances which you know about? If so, what?
- Any special events? If so, what?
- What is the person's next development step or promotion likely to be?
    - What are the key tasks for that post?
    - Which of these tasks could cause difficulty?
- What succession planning do you have?
- What are the strategic strengths of your organization?
    - What is the evidence?
- What are the strategic weaknesses of your organization?
    - What threats do these present now/in the future?
- What do you want the future to look like?
    - How do you want people to operate in the future?
- What will happen if we do nothing?
- How will we know if any training or development action is successful?
- What are your competitors doing?
- Who are your customers and how do they measure you?
    - How well do you meet your customers' requirements?
- What are your improvement targets for this year?
- Who are your best people?
- What is it these people do which impresses you?
- Knowing what you know now what do you think we should do?

Asking such questions can help you identify three types of training needs:

- *Reactive*. Where a problem exists and training is required to remove the problem.
- *Flexibility based*: Where training is needed to enable people to undertake a range of new tasks as well as their existing ones.

Participant: <u>John Brown</u>
Job Title: <u>Production Supervisor</u>   Location _____
Nominating Person/Manager: <u>Sarah Smith, Factory Manager</u>

GOAL What is this agreement about? What is the title?	IMPROVING MY LEADERSHIP SKILLS.
OBJECTIVES/COMPETENCES What knowledge do you wish to develop? What skills do you intend to develop?	1. HOW TO GIVE INSTRUCTIONS WITHOUT CAUSING OFFENCE. 2. IMPROVE MY DELEGATION SKILLS. 3. HOW TO HANDLE LOW PERFORMERS.
LEARNING PROCESS How will you achieve the objectives? What activities, experience, exercises will you carry out?	ATTEND A COURSE ON LEADERSHIP. SELF-ASSESSMENT QUESTIONNAIRES.
RESOURCES AND SUPPORT What resources could you use, eg books, video tapes, etc? What other support could be useful, eg contact with specific people?	WORK THROUGH SITUATIONAL LEADER-SHIP II SELF-STUDY PACKAGE. READ THE '1 MINUTE MANAGER'.
EVALUATION What will be the evidence to demonstrate what you have learned, eg presentation, project, questionnaire, doing it! (Each objective needs evaluating.)	1. BEFORE AND AFTER FEEDBACK FROM MY MANAGER AND TEAM. 2. TEAM MEMBERS UNDERTAKING NEW RESPONSIBILITIES. 3. MEASURABLE IMPROVED PERFORMANCE.

SUCCESS CRITERIA
What 'measures' will be used to ensure the learning has been successful –
ie, Quantitative improvement
    Qualitative improvement
    Operate in a new skill area
    Use new techniques/behaviours
    Feedback from others
	NOTICEABLE IMPROVEMENT IN TEAM RELATIONS OVER NEXT THREE MONTHS.
	
	MY SPENDING MORE TIME PLANNING AND LESS FIRE FIGHTING.
	
	15% PERFORMANCE IMPROVEMENT (AVERAGE) FROM LOW PERFORMERS.

DATE OF AGREEMENT   <u>16th July 1992</u>
COMPLETION DATE OF AGREEMENT   <u>1st October 1992</u>
Agreed: Participant's signature   <u>John Brown</u>
Nominating person's signature   <u>Sarah Smith</u>

Figure 4.2 *A sample learning agreement*

- *Developmental*: Involves training people over a period of time in readiness for a future requirement or opportunity.

One way of ensuring that the answers to any questions are satisfactory is to use a learning agreement. This is a simple document which is completed and agreed by both the learner and his/her manager. An illustration of a completed learning agreement is given in Figure 4.2.

This simple yet powerful document achieves a number of objectives:

- it ensures that a number of important answers are given to equally important questions;
- it ensures that both the learner and the manager understand what the learning assignment covers and what change or improvement is expected;
- it provides measures of improvement/change;
- it brings together both the learner and the manager to discuss development which is linked to operational performance;
- it provides an opportunity to double check the diagnosis – ie, completing the document answers the question 'Why are we doing this?';
- it provides a link between diagnosis and the learning activity.

How do I Convert Training Needs into Learning Events?

Above all, avoid being tempted to take short cuts and 'deliver training' without first discovering the real needs. Once the needs have been clarified then a whole variety of options exist:

- attending a formal training course;
- additional duties (horizontal loading) ⎫
- extra responsibilities (vertical loading) ⎬ job enrichment
- self-study material – distance learning;
- shadowing – mentoring;
- secondments – action learning;
- developing others – passing on the skills you've learnt;
- special projects;
- on-the-job training.

For detailed and accurate supporting information on these approaches please refer to other books in the Kogan Page *Practical Trainer Series*; a list appears at the front of this book.

Irrespective of which option you choose, learning events must be underpinned by a model of how people learn. In our view one of the most useful learning models for trainers is the experiential learning cycle developed originally by David Kolb. Experiential learning designs are now commonplace in the training world. Pfeiffer and Jones* suggest that:

> experiential learning occurs when a person engages in some activity, looks back at the activity critically, abstracts some useful insights from the analysis, and puts the results to work.

Kolb illustrated these ideas diagrammatically, as shown in Figure 4.3.

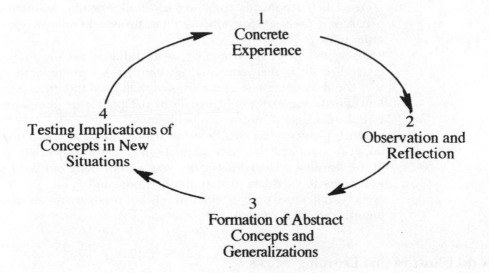

Source: Kolb *et al*, *Organizational Behaviour: An Experimental Approach*, 5/E, © 1991, p. 59. Reprinted by permission of Prentice-Hall, Englewood Cliffs, NJ

Figure 4.3 *The experiential learning cycle*

When applied to training situations this cycle suggests that it is usually best to start the process of learning with some kind of relevant experience. For example, if we were helping a manager to examine and modify his/her management style we would start with an experience (ie, exercise, simulation, live practice etc) which allowed the manager to practise

---

* Pfeiffer, JW and Jones, JE (1980) 'Fleshing in the Experiential Learning Cycle', in Pfeiffer, JW and Jones, JE, *Annual Handbook for Group Facilitators*, University Associates Inc.

and gather information about their current style. That is, starting from the manager's perspective rather than our own as trainers.

Next we would encourage the manager to reflect on, and discuss how they had acted:

- what they were seeking to do (ie, their goal);
- what outcomes they expected;
- how they felt during the process;
- what implications were involved;
- how their actions fit with any models or theories they currently know about management style.

The intention at this stage would be to help the manager begin to make sense of their actions and come to a new understanding about how they behave – if necessary introducing them to new theories or models in order to help.

Using this new understanding, stage three allows the manager to generalize about alternative management styles together with options they could try out. These options would then need thorough consideration to make sure they would actually help. Finally stage three would end with the manager planning new behaviour.

Once planning was complete the manager could then test out the implications of what they have learned – in so doing completing one loop of the learning cycle. However the very act of testing out the learning would give further data to start another loop, and so on. The learning cycle is an iterative process which slowly but surely moves an individual towards their desired goal.

How do I Ensure that Learning 'Sticks'?

The third stage in the TQM learning process is ensuring that the learning 'sticks'. Irrespective of which development method was chosen in stage two it will be useless unless the learning is applied back in the workplace. In a sense this should follow from the experiential learning cycle. The final stage of the cycle – application – is not only application as part of a training event but also application in the workplace. However, many learning events take place in off-the-job settings and by definition the environment in such settings will be different to the workplace. This does not mean that off-the-job training is unrealistic, it simply means that the workplace is unique. This uniqueness could be the result of a combination of factors:

- different physical environment;
- different people;
- different pressure or stressors;
- different routines;
- the boss back in the workplace manages differently to how the trainer coaches.

All of these factors could 'get in the way' so that learning is not easily transferred back to the workplace. We would therefore suggest that:

- where possible use the workplace as the centre of learning – problems with transfer are then circumvented;
- where this is not possible and the training takes place elsewhere then we need to take this into account and help with the transfer of learning and/or skills back to the workplace.

In other words, we need to help 'make it stick'.

Where training is carried out off-the-job then a number of different techniques can be used to assist transfer; these include:

- making sure all the learner's colleagues are briefed before the training so that they know who is going, why, when, and what is expected when the learner returns;
- on returning, the learner can give a 'mini teach-in' to his/her colleagues;
- where team briefing is used, 'What training is taking place?' could be included as an agenda item;
- when a manager notices colleagues asking questions and showing interest in a learner's experience then he/she can acknowledge/reward such behaviour; However, where they notice chastizing or devaluing behaviour he/she can confront it;
- after training the learner could write a short summary of the main points of the training and this could be put on the notice board;
- in team meetings the team leader should show positive support for the training and also highlight the operational improvements and benefits;
- the manager could develop his/her own coaching skills in order to provide more support for learners;
- in team meetings ensure that training is not the last agenda item;
- previous learners can be used to help run further training workshops;
- where company newsletters or house magazines are circulated, ensure that training together with photographs of trainees are a regular feature;

- display prominently charts, graphs and skills matrices showing the pace of training and who is competent at what;
- ensure that company training policy refers to line managers' performance being evaluated in terms of both departmental efficiency and other criteria such as:
  - feedback concerning the interest shown in employees (easily collected by using a questionnaire)
  - the number of learning agreements per employee per year
  - how much time is logged in diaries for debriefing and reviewing learners' progress
  - changes/improvements in operational routines and practices due to employees' involvement in development programmes;
- ensure that all learners are debriefed by their manager on return to work.

If we were to select only one of these ideas for assisting the transfer of learning back into the workplace it would be adequate debriefing by the manager on the learner's return to work. All too often debriefing is left to chance and in many instances it does not take place at all. In our view debriefing is essential. In view of this we will outline further the steps in the debriefing process. To be effective, debriefing involves five main stages.

Stage 1: Preparation

Formalize the event – prepare the learner and let them know:

- why you want the debriefing meeting to take place;
- where and when the meeting will take place;
- that you (ie, the manager) will be referring to the learning agreement;
- that you will be very interested in what the learner has to say about the development experience.

Stage 2: Introduction

Start off with icebreaking questions aimed at getting the learner to feel as comfortable as possible. Questions might include:

- How did it go?
- What was the course like?
- What was included in the training?

or any other vague, non-specific prompts.

Stage 3: Gathering Information

Aim to obtain clear accurate statements about the learning; questions could include:
- What did you learn about?
- What were the most interesting aspects of ...?
- ... Why was that?
- Where did you experience the most difficulty?

Stage 4: Application

This is very closely linked to the learning agreement. In this stage attempt to gain explicit understanding and agreement about where and when the new skill or knowledge will be used. Also recognize that application back at work can be difficult – reach agreement on how you can support or assist the learner. Useful questions include:

- How do you intend to use the new knowledge/skill?
- What will you be doing differently?
- What support do you want from me?
- How will we recognize change/improvement?
- How can I help you apply the learning successfully?

Stage 5: Measurement

This is also closely linked to the learning agreement. In this stage both the manager and the learner re-examine the measures in the learning agreement and test to see if they are still realistic. Useful questions include:
- How will you demonstrate that the training has been successful?
- How will I/others see the effect of this training?
- What sort of timescale are we talking about for change/improvement to be fully implemented?

TRAINER'S TIP

In our experience 'making it stick' is a critical part of the learning process. Traditionally it is the one where the least amount of energy and effort is invested. However, with TQM trainers must actively support learners as they re-enter their normal workplace.

Do remember – debriefing has to be carried out by the manager; your role as the trainer is to support the manager, ie, helping them acquire the skills needed to carry out effective debriefings.

How do I Evaluate Training?

Evaluating training has been a perennial problem. However, in TQM the only forms of evaluation which really matter are the customer's. For training in a TQM setting there are at least two customers:

Customer 1: the learner or recipient of the training.
Customer 2: the recipient of the effect of the training – usually the learner's manager.

It follows therefore that training and development will have at least two sets of customer success criteria to take into account. We will address each of these separately.

Customer 1: The Learner's Evaluation:

In TQM it is important to clarify the expectations of the learner at the start of any training process. This will form the basis of the evaluation. It also provides the trainer with the opportunity to question and clarify the learner's expectations. Where any expectations appear unreasonable or outside of the brief of a learning event they can be discussed openly with the learner and if necessary modified.

As the training progresses, periodically review progress against the learner's original expectations. This means soliciting feedback. Periodic reviews are essential as these give you the opportunity to take corrective action if needed.

At the end of the training, once more refer the learner back to their original expectations and ask them to comment on how closely their expectations were met.

TRAINER'S TIP

The following questions may be of value in an end-of-course review:

Venue: What are your views on the standard of accommodation/facilities? What improvements could be made?

Trainers: What are your views on the standard of the training you have received? Did you feel confident in the ability of the trainers? What improvements could be made?

Content and material: What are your views on how the course was structured and the quality of any material/aids used? What improvements could be made?

Impact of training: In what ways has this course affected you? How will it influence how you work and/or what you do in the future? What improvements could be made?

Relevance: How relevant was this training for you?

Any other comments:

Customer 2: The Manager's Evaluation (usually)

The manager will be interested in the effect of any training back in the workplace. It follows, therefore, that this is how they will evaluate the effectiveness of both the training and the trainer. The manager's actual evaluation criteria should always be stated on any learning agreement. This will then double as a statement about 'why we are doing the training in the first place'.

The following list gives a few examples of actual evaluation criteria used by managers in a few of our client companies:

- Improvement in response time.
- Ability to carry out new tasks to predetermined standards.
- Reduction in material wastage.
- Reduction in sickness and/or absenteeism.
- Improved staff retention.
- Improved unit and/or individual efficiency levels.
- Reduction in machine down-time.
- Improvement in the quality of the product.
- Improved financial performance.
- Projected cash savings.
- The adoption of different/improved routines and processes.

In our view these types of criteria are more useful (and more demanding) than traditional training criteria such as:

- Improve delegate's skill.
- Better first-line supervision.
- Improve communication.
- Develop greater flexibility.

When TQM training and development are evaluated we must ensure it is against customer's criteria and not the trainer's, and as often as possible expressed in terms of real business performance indicators.

TRAINER'S TIP

If you are ever asked why line managers should spend time on evaluation, consider the following. Evaluation is important to:

- demonstrate that the training and the needs analysis were accurate;
- confirm to the manager that the money was well spent;
- give the learner feedback which demonstrates that they are capable and have achieved higher/improved levels of performance.

Wherever possible graph or chart performance improvements. This will provide motivation to continue investing in training.

QUESTIONS FOR THE TQM TRAINER

- How is training perceived in your organization?
- What can you do to persuade managers that training is a process which is their responsibility rather than an event for which you are responsible?
- How can you help your colleagues in training come to terms with the view that line managers need to be more involved in the whole training process?
- What training activities are you involved with which could be modified to be more experiential and learner-centred?
- What opportunities exist for you to introduce learning agreements?
- What can you do to ensure that newly acquired skills are transferred and applied in the workplace?
- What percentage of time is spent on the four stages of the learning process? Is this division appropriate?
- How is training evaluated in your organization? Is this compatible with the requirements of TQM?
- How does what you do differ from what has been discussed in this chapter?

5 The Business Improvement Process

▷ SUMMARY ◁

- The Business Improvement Process (BIP) is the framework on which the TQM organization develops.
- The senior management team must map out the high-level process chart collaboratively.
- The needs of the external customer and the evaluation criteria must be agreed explicitly – these will change over time.
- Cascading the BIP simultaneously extends the internal supplier/customer network.
- Customer requirements, key tasks and measures must be documented.
- Everyone should fully understand their role and where they fit in the process.
- Maximize value-adding activities and minimize non-value-adding activities.
- The supplier/customer chain can be used to develop continuous improvement.
- Working in a supplier/customer relationship requires different attitudes and behaviour to working in a boss/subordinate relationship.
- The cost of quality is a powerful way to achieve continuous improvement and unit cost reduction – an open and supportive environment is essential.

What is the Business Improvement Process?

Rarely if ever do we come across a situation where there is only one way to do something. TQM is no different. The Business Improvement Process (BIP) is one approach to developing a TQM framework which has proven itself in a number of organizations. Primarily the BIP is the organizational structure on which TQM is built. However, it is much more than a family tree or wall chart. It is a series of interlinking frameworks and systems which are all the product of TQM beliefs and methodology. Hence, the objectives of the BIP are the same as those of TQM:

> To meet the needs of the customer consistently, while at the same time achieving continuous improvement in all activities.

Your role as a TQM trainer requires that you understand these concepts thoroughly yourself and enable your customers (ie, managers and employees in the organization) to interpret and apply them in the workplace.

This chapter will examine these frameworks and systems one at a time. However, you must appreciate that their application is not a linear process as the layout of the chapter may suggest. The frameworks and systems may overlap with each other, or operate in series. Furthermore, their application and rate of success is a product of the prevailing management style and culture of the organization.

EXERCISE: THINKING TQM

Assume for a minute that as consultants we are visiting your organization for the first time and you have been selected to show us around. As part of our investigation we would ask you the following question:

> 'To help us understand your company better, would you draw on a piece of paper how you think your company is organized?'

Try to answer this question on a separate sheet of paper, then compare your response with ours. If your diagram is similar to the organizational pyramid in Figure 5.1 then the following discussion may be of interest.

When managers in traditional organizations are asked to complete this exercise they normally respond by drawing a pyramid with the chief executive (or chairperson) at the top, the board members underneath then the senior managers, middle managers, supervisors and so on. This gives us an insight into their perception of the values and focus on which the organization operates.

This is not the occasion to discuss in depth the relationship between thoughts and behaviour; suffice to say that if we think consistently in a certain way then over time we are likely to behave in a similar manner.

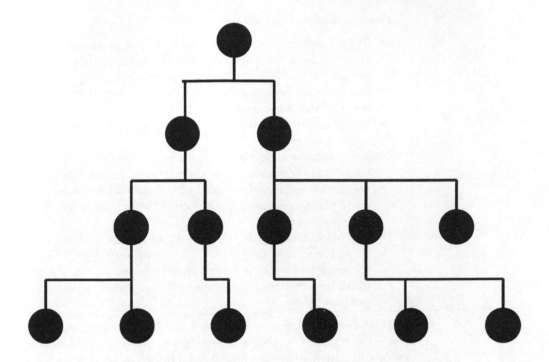

Figure 5.1 *The organizational pyramid*

This is an example of the Pygmalion Effect in management. Consequently, if a group of managers think about running a business in a certain way then it is highly likely that the business will operate in that way. If this is the case then it makes sense to ensure that their thoughts and ideas support TQM. To check this out we need to ask whether a pyramid structure take us closer to or further away from the vision.

To answer this question we need to think about how far a pyramid structure supports TQM. You might like to think about this in terms of advantages and disadvantages and list your ideas on a separate sheet. When you have done this compare your response with ours below.

The *advantages* include:

- everyone knows who their boss is and accountability is clear;
- the structure facilitates quick communication from top to bottom and vice- versa;
- the structure provides a sense of security – everyone knows their location.

The *disadvantages* include:

- TQM emphasizes the importance of customers but they are not represented in the pyramid. Does this indicate they are central or peripheral to the organization's existence?
- the pyramid does not help anyone understand how work flows through the organization;
- the pyramid does not show how one department supports or services others;
- the emphasis is clearly on who is in charge of whom. This could support and consolidate an authoritative/punitive environment;
- it does not encourage people in the organization to give feedback, particularly those near the bottom – this is critical for continuous improvement;
- it reinforces sluggish transfer of information. The designated route for transferring information is up one department's management structure and then down another. This will inhibit a quick response and undermine success where 'time-based' competition exists.

In TQM a pyramid structure is limited in value. However, in our view it is always likely to be necessary to some degree, particularly in large organizations. As a structure it may have helped Julius Caesar control his legions (and make immense territorial gains) but it does not lend itself with equal success to running a business where the objectives are about meeting the needs of customers and achieving continuous improvement. For this we need something different – in TQM this is the BIP.

Developing a BIP starts with getting people to think differently – outside of the traditions and limitations of the pyramid and more towards process management.

What is process management?

Process management is a way of looking at how a business is managed. In addition it makes significant improvements in getting everyone to be accountable for the quality of their own work.

To demonstrate what we mean, we will show how a process management chart was created with the senior management team of a successful manufacturing business. Later in the chapter we will also give examples from other types of organizations.

BIP Stage 1a

First of all, confirm that you have a customer(s) for your products. Then determine which function or department is responsible for working closely with the customer. In our case this was the sales and design department. Their primary role was to secure orders/sales.

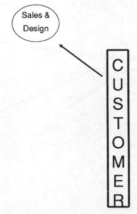

Figure 5.2 *BIP stage 1a*

Note: like all other relationships, the relationship between sales and design and the customer requires extensive two-way communication – the purpose here was to secure orders, and therefore the arrow in Figure 5.2 points in one direction only.

BIP Stage 1b

Once orders were received by the sales and design department, this information was passed to the production planning department.

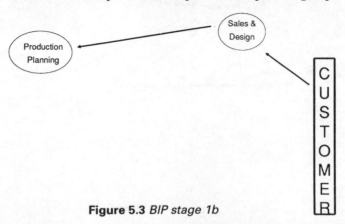

Figure 5.3 *BIP stage 1b*

BIP Stage 1c

The role of production planning was to coordinate purchasing of raw materials and synchronize material deliveries with manufacturing. They also carried out advance planning for deliveries from the warehouse to the customer. To do all this they fed information to the purchasing, production and warehouse departments.

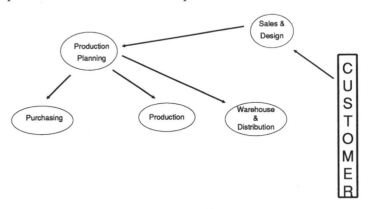

Figure 5.4 *BIP stage 1c*

BIP Stage 1d

The purchasing department then needed to order and receive all raw materials from external suppliers. Once received, the raw materials could be fed to the production department.

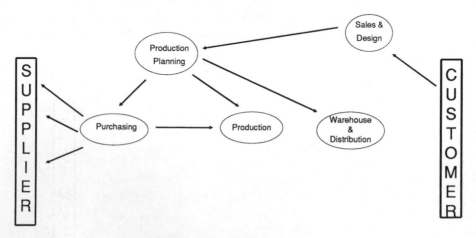

Figure 5.5 *BIP stage 1d*

BIP Stage 1e

The production department then made the products and handed them on to the warehouse and distribution departments. In accordance with an agreed 'Delivery to Customer Schedule' the warehouse and distribution department despatched and delivered the finished goods.

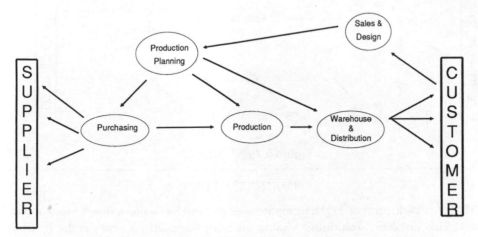

Figure 5.6 *BIP stage 1e*

BIP Stage 1f

Finally, a number of services provided continuous support for this process. They included:

Personnel: recruitment, employee welfare, etc.
Information technology: computer system maintenance and development.
Finance: wages, cost control and financing.
Industrial engineering: setting operational values and assisting in organizing workflow.

The resulting process chart is illustrated in Figure 5.7.

This is referred to as a 'high-level process chart'. Each of the departments shown on the chart are represented by a senior manager/executive in the board room or the highest level of autonomous decision-making.

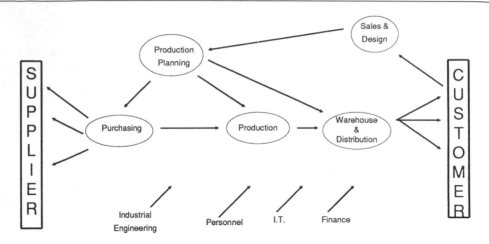

Figure 5.7 *BIP stage 1f*

TRAINER'S TIP

With the introduction of TQM, in many cases you will be challenging the way people think. This involves questioning what many have accepted for years as the truth or the way things are done. Be careful to avoid using expressions like 'the right way' and 'the wrong way'. This will only create defensiveness. An alternative approach could be to recognize that the needs of tomorrow are different to the needs of yesterday and therefore a different approach needs to be considered.

Figure 5.7 (the process management chart) differs considerably from the pyramid we examined earlier. One of the major differences is that with the process chart we can clearly see how information/work moves through the organization, ie, from one department (supplier) downstream to the next (its customer) who then in turn becomes a supplier to their customer department. On paper we now have an internal supplier/ customer chain.

TRAINER'S TIP

In the pyramid, the most important person anyone must satisfy is the boss. With process management the most important person is the customer (both internal and external). This needs continuous reinforcement.

94

Who is Responsible for the BIP?

With the BIP the chief executive is the 'process owner' and is responsible for the complete process. However, they are not shown on the high-level chart. This is because:

- unless they also have some functional responsibility they are not part of the supplier/customer chain;
- if the chief executive were shown this may reinforce his/her position in the organization as the decision-maker which would work against the TQM ethic of empowering others;
- they are not as important as customers.

Nevertheless, the role of the process owner is critical. Through appropriate direction, role modelling, encouragement and patience, he/she will contribute immensely to the successful implementation of TQM.

How do we Create and Implement the BIP?

Creating and implementing the BIP is a process which involves considerable detail. To keep our explanation simple we have divided the process into eight sequential stages:

BIP Stage 1: Creating the High-level Process Chart

The high-level process chart is initially created by the senior management team. To do this they will need to work together collaboratively and agree the various supplier/customer chains throughout the organization (as outlined in the previous section on process management). Your role involves making sure they understand the concepts of a high-level process chart and supplier/customer chain and facilitating their subsequent discussion.

TRAINER'S TIP

When working together to create the process chart, the senior team may require help and will need a few attempts to get the diagram sufficiently correct for all department heads to 'buy into it'. This may take some time.

Do not underestimate the necessity for the chart to be developed collaboratively between the senior team. If coercion is used you can guarantee the emerging BIP will fail. As the trainer you are well placed to guide and facilitate the discussion.

BIP Stage 2: Agreeing External Customer Requirements

In Chapter 1 we asked 'How do we measure the organization's performance?' and answered – 'The same way the customer does'. This is not meant to be a glib comment but a point of strategic importance. It is essential that your organization obtains explicit understanding and agreement about your customers' requirements. This means talking to them and (more importantly) listening to what they have to say. However, before starting to collect customer data it is important to consider a few basic points:

Use an agreed format and document it – spend time deciding what questions are going to be asked and how the replies will be recorded. It is important to have a standard method of recording otherwise comparing one customer's response with another (or one customer with his/her previous response) becomes a problem.

Keep it simple – make it easy for the customer to feel comfortable with this approach; this will also enable your representative to use it with confidence.

Ensure the exercise can be repeated – collecting data is not a one-off exercise. Successful organizations stay very close to what their customers want – they continually solicit feedback.

Use competent people – collecting unbiased data is a skilled activity which needs to be handled with care, particularly if the data are of a sensitive nature, eg, 'how a customer feels'.

To carry out a supplier/customer interview effectively your representative will need to be:

- assertive, a good listener and good at asking questions;
- credible with the customer;
- knowledgeable about your product/service;
- good at organizing information;
- sensitive to feelings (their own and others) and able to discuss emotive issues and relationships openly.

When collecting customer data we prefer to use a standard single sheet questionnaire such as illustrated in Figure 5.8

TRAINER'S TIP

Many organizations use external consultants for the data collection process. This ensures that it is untainted by 'insider interpretation'. Furthermore, people often find it easier to talk to a third party. However, if internal staff are used for this purpose there are probably training implications for them to develop the necessary skills.

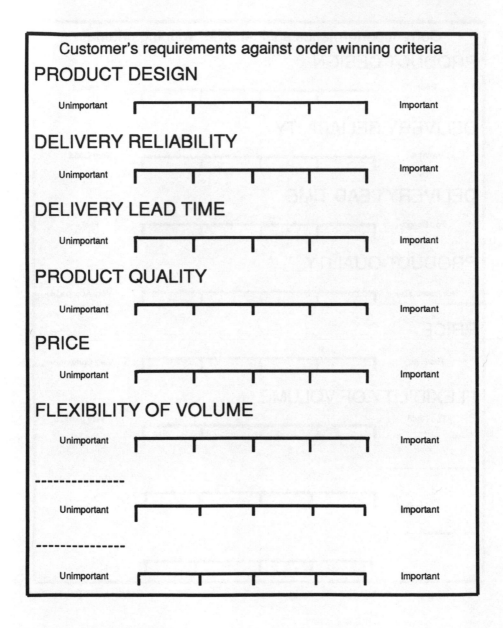

Figure 5.8 *Customer's requirements – order-winning criteria*

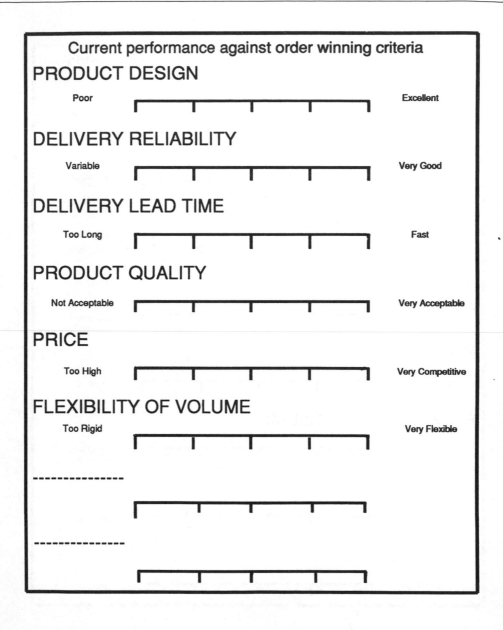

Figure 5.9 *Current performance questionnaire – possible order-losing criteria*

The left-hand side of this questionnaire shows the various criteria which the customer has indicated are of importance. Also, blanks are included at the bottom for the customer to specify any other particular requirements.

As well as understanding the customer's requirements, you can also take the opportunity to find out how well your organization is currently performing. To help with this we have included a second questionnaire specifically for this purpose (see Figure 5.9)

You will note that the two questionnaires in Figures 5.8 and 5.9 will overlay one another. This allows you to see at a glance not only the relative importance of the customer's criteria but also how well you are doing on each of them. This makes it a lot easier to identify where you need to improve.

TRAINER'S TIP

The success of your organization will be in direct proportion to how closely you meet your customers' requirements (including shareholders). This in turn will be reflected in how frequently you ask 'How well are we doing?'

It is important to recognize that perception is more important than reality. In other words, if a customer's evaluation of your performance is poor and yet you have evidence to suggest they are wrong, then simply confronting them with your evidence is not a good idea. It may take longer, but as an alternative try working on changing their perception – this leaves the customer's self-image intact.

Once you have agreed the customer's requirements (for the present), these can be put into the high-level process chart as shown in Figure 5.10.

In our discussion so far our illustrations of high-level process charts have been for a manufacturing business. We have therefore included two others: Figure 5.11 which is based on a domestic appliance sales and service organization., and Figure 5.12 which is based on a mail order company.

Note: all our examples of high-level process charts are deliberately generic. We do not advise you to try to impose them on your organization. By all means use them as models but it is essential that you help your senior managers create their own.

Where an organization has more than one type of customer for which the internal process varies (eg, supplying gas, electricity or water to domestic customers could be different from supplying industrial customers) it is often sensible to draw the process charts separately for each customer group. The two may be overlaid to give the total picture.

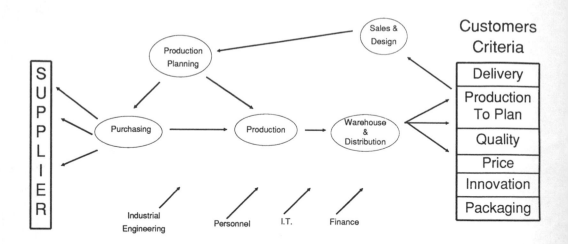

Focus on the Process or Flow of Information/Work

Figure 5.10 *BIP high-level process chart in manufacturing*

TRAINER'S TIP

Some organizations fail to regard their shareholders or holding company as customers. This could prove fatal. You must pay close attention to the needs of holding company directors as well as meeting the needs of those who buy your product. For example, directors might not always wish to focus on profit – reducing stock or generating cash flow could be two other requirements. You need to be equally clear on these requirements as this will influence what you do. As a trainer part of your role is to influence this.

If your first impression is that high-level process charts are rather simple – we would agree. They *are* simple. At a high level it is important to make the internal supplier/customer chain as clear and obvious as possible.

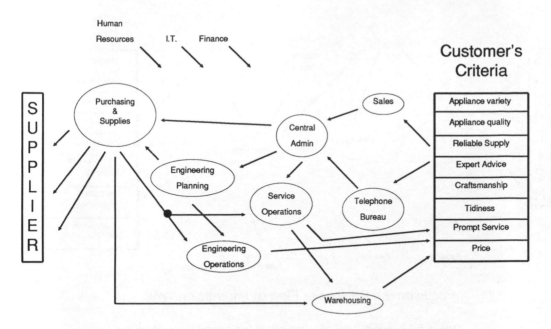

Focus on the Process or Flow of Information/Work

Figure 5.11 *High-level process chart for a sales and service organization*

TRAINER'S TIP

When you first introduce the concept of process management to your managers, do not be surprised if their comments are, 'We do that anyway', or 'Yes we know that, we've been doing it for years'.

We assure you that if you ask them individually to draw the process for the company you will be presented with a rich variety of diagrams.

BIP Stage 3: Determining High-level Internal Supplier/Customer Requirements

Once you have mapped out the high-level chart and determined your external customer's requirements, it is time for the senior managers of all departments represented on the chart to hold their own supplier/customer reviews with each other. The purpose of the reviews is for each internal customer to agree clearly what is required of their supplier.

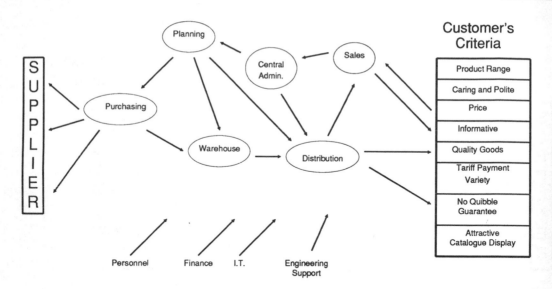

Focus on the Process or Flow of Information/Work

Figure 5.12 *High-level process chart for a mail order company*

Furthermore, it is also very important for them to agree how performance will be measured. The following guidelines could prove helpful:

- keep department-on-department measures down to an absolute minimum – one being ideal;
- remember the whole purpose of the review is based on the belief that 'the only way you can consistently meet the needs of the external customer is by consistently meeting the needs of internal customers' – hence is is imperative the reviews are carried out thoroughly;
- align all activities and measures with meeting the explicit requirements of the external customer;
- ensure all agreed activities and measures are stretching (but achievable). Where the supplier and customer fail to agree, then the process owner may need to intervene – not to vote in favour of one side or the other, but to explore the validity of the customer's request and also the difficulties which are preventing the supplier confirming agreement.

BIP Stage 4: Agreeing High-level Supplier/Customer Measures with the Process Owner

After the supplier/customer measures have been identified for every link in the high-level supplier/customer chain, the senior management team should meet again with the process owner to discuss:

- are they feasible?
- are they challenging or too easy?
- collectively do they ensure that the organization meets the needs of the external customer?

The process owner must agree to the measures or have them adjusted. These are the measures for which he/she will be accountable, not only to the customer but also to the shareholders and the employees of the organization (through success or failure).

As an illustration of the process so far, consider Figures 5.11 and 5.13. Figure 5.11 illustrates a high-level process chart for a sales and service organization; Figure 5.13 shows a selection from the high-level supplier/ customer agreement schedule from the same organization.

Supplier	Customer	Customer Measures
Sales	Central Administration	* Timely supply of new sales information * Number of changes against forecast
Central Administration	Purchasing and Supplies	* Number of Consumable Requisitions per month * Timely supply of information * Number of queries on information received
	Engineering Planning	* Number of jobs completed as per the plan * Number of queries regarding computer data * Accuracy of computer records
	Service Operations	* Accuracy of computer records * Number of jobs completed as planned
Telephone Bureau	Central Administration	* Accuracy of computer data on job and customer
Engineering Planning	Engineering Operations	* Number of jobs completed as planned * Number of 'return to depot' calls for materials
Service Operations	Warehouse	* 24hr delivery notice required * Initiate monthly performance reviews

Figure 5.13 *Internal supplier/customer departmental requirements*

BIP Stage 5: Reaching Departmental Agreement and Allocating Key Tasks and Activities

After the process owner has agreed the high-level supplier/customer measures, each department head should meet with his/her team of managers and/or senior members of staff and:

- outline the supplier/customer process;
- clarify the BIP chart;
- explain the external customer's requirements and also give information on current performance levels;
- state the measures agreed with their internal customers;
- state the requirements/measures agreed with their internal supplier.

We would suggest that under the leadership of the department head, the team now needs to work through the following issues and make proposals:

- Why do we exist? (A departmental mission statement.)
- What activities do we (the department) need to perform in order to meet our internal customer's high-level measures?
- Which one of us will be responsible for each of these activities? Then allocate them.

Allocating the activities is obviously important as a capable and willing person is much more likely to ensure success than someone who is coerced into the role. You might also like to think through what criteria should be used when allocating key tasks/activities. We would include:

- previous experience of the activity;
- who has the knowledge;
- number of people in the department;
- location;
- career development;
- desire to do it.

This list can be used objectively to determine who is best suited to a particular task based on who meets the most criteria.

Following this it is important to ensure that all actions progressively 'add value', ie, actions are undertaken because:

They are necessary
to
complete an activity
to
provide your internal customer with a service
which
meets a predetermined standard
which
is essential to help provide the external customer
with
what they want.

BIP Stage 6: Agreeing the Detail of the Customer's Activity Measures

As the next step, each designated activity holder meets with the actual customer of that activity; by this we mean the specific individual(s) who receive the 'work done'. This could be other people within the same department or members of another department. Figure 5.14 shows an actual customer/supplier chain in a production department which is currently working with TQM; Figure 5.15 shows an overview of this supplier/customer review process.

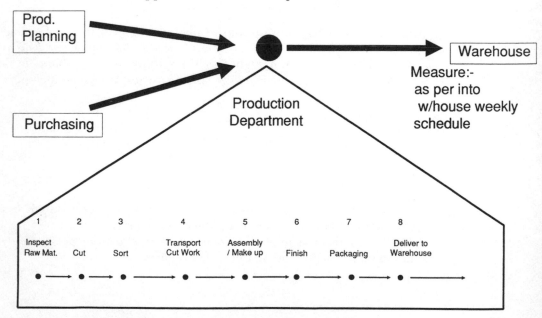

Figure 5.14 *Customer/Supplier chain in a production department*

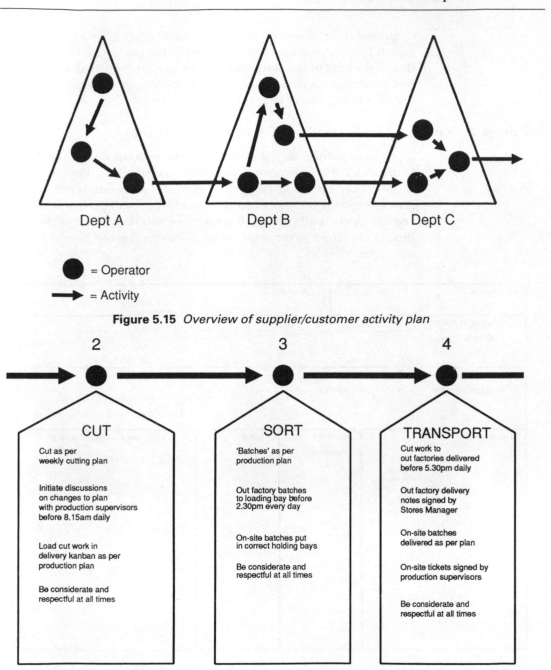

Figure 5.15 *Overview of supplier/customer activity plan*

Figure 5.16 *Level of detail needed between supplier and customer*

During these meetings the activity holder needs to agree in detail exactly how the customer will measure his/her performance. An illustration of the level of detail needed is given in Figure 5.16. All the information generated needs to be recorded. A typical format for this is shown in Figure 5.17 with notes for guidance in Figure 5.18.

BIP Stage 7: Confirming Understanding of Activities and Measures

The activity holders should now meet again with the departmental head to share all the information they have gathered on their respective activities, the intention being that they all fully understand both the activities and the measures agreed. Once more the department head can take the opportunity to ask, 'If we achieve success with all of these, will this take us closer to or further away from meeting the agreed needs of our customer?'.

1 DEPARTMENT	2 CUSTOMER		3 DATE
4 DEPARTMENT PURPOSE (Why do we exsist?)			
5 CUSTOMER'S REQUIREMENTS AND SUCCESS CRITERIA			
6 ACTIVITIES	7 ACTIVITY'S CUSTOMER	8 ACTIVITY HOLDER	9 CUSTOMER'S MEASURE OF ACTIVITY

Figure 5.17 *Document to record supplier/customer activities*

1. State name of own department.

2. What is the name of the internal department which is your customer? Where there is more than one internal customer a separate form should be used for each internal customer department.

3. Date this form was completed.

4. In relation to the customer stated above, what purpose do we serve, why do we exist? (A mini mission statement.)

5. Keeping to no more than two or three (preferably just one) state the requirement(s) of your customer and also how they (customer) will measure your (department) performance.

   Note: Each separate requirement must have a separate measure.

6. Looking at the customer requirement(s) stated above, what activities must take place in order to satisfy these requirement(s)?

7. Who is the particular (name) customer of the activity stated? This may include customers within your own department as well as those from outside.

8. Which person in your department is to be accountable for successfully completing this activity?

9. From discussion between the activity holder and the activity's customer what is the explicit agreed measure of this activity?

Final Check

If all these activities are carried out and meet their individual customers measure, will this ensure that the requirement(s) (see 5) will be met?

Figure 5.18 *Recording supplier/customer activities – notes for guidance*

TRAINER'S TIP

Do not allow the allocation of activities to be seen as an abdication of involvement or support by others. Individuals in all corners of the department must be able to contribute towards attainment of the agreed measures.

SUPPLIER
(Dept.) Purchasing

CUSTOMER
(Dept.) Production

Date

Please rate the following Activities in two ways:
    1 Rate the activity on our current performance
    2 Rate the importance of the activity to you

KEY ACTIVITIES	1 (0-10)	2 (0-10)
1 TO PROVIDE MATERIALS	5	10
2 TO PROVIDE SPECIFICATIONS	9	6
3 TO PRODUCE DELIVERY SCHEDULES	7	7
4 TO PROVIDE MATERIAL AVAILABILITY INFORMATION	5	8
5 TO PROVIDE LEADTIMES ON UNCONFIRMED ORDERS	9	5
6 --------------------		

Figure 5.19 *Activity performance survey*

BIP Stage 8: Agreeing which Activities have Priority

During the early stages of TQM do remember that there is still a business to run. It will probably be inappropriate to invest all the talent, skill and resources available in all activities simultaneously. Therefore it will be important to prioritize activities and decide which to work on first.

A successful customer-centred way of doing this is to get the customer to allocate priorities for you. Figure 5.19 is a simple questionnaire which was used for this purpose with one of our client companies. In this instance the purchasing manager asked the production manager (his customer) to complete the form.

As you can see from the information given, the purchasing department:

Needed to improve on
– activity 1: providing materials
– activity 4: providing material availability information.
Was performing well on
– activity 3: producing delivery schedules.
Was over-performing on
– activity 2: providing specification
– activity 5: providing lead times on unconfirmed orders.

Note: over-performing is the equivalent of waste and should be addressed.

The cascade process outlined in BIP Stages 1 to 8 needs to be continued right through the organization. As this happens and as lower levels of the organization become involved, the information they are given will change. Operational staff, shop floor, clerical and manual employees need to know specifically about their own roles and their immediate suppliers and customers. Later on all groups will both want and need to know about more distant parts of the organization. However, during the early stages this is unlikely to be the case.

A good indicator of success with the BIP cascade is when everyone in the organization can confidently and accurately complete the simple check-sheet shown in Figure 5.20.

What are Order-winning Criteria?

Order-winning criteria are what your customers use to evaluate your performance. Customer satisfaction depends on meeting the order-win-

NAME .... DATE ....

JOB TITLE ....

DEPARTMENT ....

MY KEY ACTIVITIES ARE ....
....
....

THEY ADD VALUE BY ....
....

MY CUSTOMERS (INTERNAL AND EXTERNAL) ARE ....
....

MY CUSTOMERS MEASURE ME BY ....
....
....

MY SUPPLIERS (INTERNAL AND EXTERNAL) ARE ....
....
....

I MEASURE MY SUPPLIERS BY ....
....
....

Figure 5.20 *What is my role in this process?*

ning criteria. This principle applies equally to meeting the needs of both internal and external customers. Unfortunately, customers are often unaware they even have order-winning criteria until they find they are dissatisfied. For example, have you ever visited a restaurant and:

- Were kept waiting at the reception desk, not because the reception staff were busy, but because there was nobody there to receive you?
- Found your soup was not as hot as you would have liked?
- Found the centre of your bread roll was still frozen?
- Had to wait just a little too long between courses?
- Found the salt cellar was empty?
- Found the roast chicken you ordered smaller than you would have liked?

All of these events happened during one evening to one of the authors. However, before arriving at a restaurant most people would not consciously think, 'Now I want to be greeted promptly and shown straight to a table. The soup should be very hot and the bread roll completely defrosted. Oh, and I'm not prepared to wait more than six and a half minutes between courses and I expect the roast chicken to cover half the plate. Also, the salt cellar should be full'.

Yet the absence of these services had implications. The customer could have felt anything from disappointment to extreme anger. Of one thing we can be sure, the restaurant will not see that customer again. But that is not where the story ends. This one customer may tell between 5 and 10 others, some of whom will also give the restaurant a wide berth as a result. Furthermore, it is also likely that at least 25 more will find out via small talk in the office, pub or at a party.

You might think this is an example which is confined solely to external customers. However, in our experience it can frequently be a feature of internal supplier/customer relations. If an internal supplier, for whatever reason (including ignorance), provides a substandard service or product then his/her customer will develop strong feelings and opinions about the supplier, particularly if the error occurs more than once. Their relationship may deteriorate to the point where they do not cooperate, become obstructive or avoid one another. The result is that the organization's ability to respond to the external customer is severely diminished. As a consequence, they might fail to satisfy the external customer's order-winning criteria and the business is taken elsewhere. It is no good relying on the knowledge that you have met the needs of the customer in the past – it is the future which counts.

You don't steer a ship by looking at its wake.

113

The moral of this is that everyone must stay close to their customer and work hard to help the customer understand their own requirements. To do this effectively you will probably need to help the customer express their order-winning criteria in an objective way which you can both measure. If you glance back at Figures 5.13 and 5.16 you will find that most of the criteria mentioned in those illustrations are objective and measurable. Therefore when working with customers it is important to use words like:

Delivery accuracy		Satisfaction
Cost		'It feels right'
Quantity		Happiness
Length		'It looks right'
Volume	Rather than	'It works okay'
Frequency		Pleasure
Weight		
Speed of Response		

What is Meant by Value-adding Activities and How can they be Quantified?

The term 'value-adding' has been mentioned previously, but what does it mean? Consider the following formula:

Total Work Effort = Value-adding Activities + Non-value-adding Activities

$$(TWE) = (VA) + (NVA)$$

In any organization the total human effort that is available is made up of value-adding components, ie, time, effort and energy spent on doing things which benefit the customers (including shareholders); and non-value-adding components, ie, time, effort and energy spent doing things from which the customers (including shareholders) derive no benefit.

With TQM the intention is to minimize (and where possible eliminate) non-value-adding effort (redefined as waste), and maximize on value-adding effort.

Value-adding activities include:	*Non-value-adding activities include:*
Getting it right first time	Error creation
Error prevention	Error inspection
Quality improvement	Error correction
Focused training	Time wasting
	Checking

No doubt you can think of more examples of VA and NVA activities which are particular to your own department. Indeed it would be time well spent if you were to think about this now!

Following identification of VA and NVA activities the next question to answer is, 'What proportion of our time do we spend on these activities?' Clearly, the more that time is spent on NVA activities the more likely we are to fail to:

- meet the needs of the customer;
- improve the service we offer;
- achieve continuous improvement;
- eliminate waste;
- reduce costs.

It is therefore imperative that you, your colleagues and your customers carry out a time analysis to determine how effectively time is being spent in your organization.

TRAINER'S TIP

VA analysis is a very powerful way of helping managers and staff. When carried out honestly it graphically illustrates how much waste managers and staff can create. However, the exercise is purely a data collection activity and should not be used in a judgemental, blaming or threatening manner – this will only succeed in getting people to disguise the truth.

If carried out regularly, the analysis will enable both you and your customer to record the amount of VA and NVA time spent. This can be plotted to form the basis of a continuous improvement chart.

This exercise is particularly useful in support or service environments as these are not usually subjected to as stringent performance controls as production units.

Paying attention to how people spend their time is a guaranteed way of achieving continuous improvement in how people, departments or the organization perform.

How does the BIP Help to Achieve Continuous Improvement?

Chapter 1 pointed out that TQM requires total involvement by everyone; this is part of the formula for continuous improvement. However, improvements with TQM are incremental and frequent. The organization becomes structured to enable and gain excitement from small gains made by anyone and everyone. The intention is to see regular 1 per cent improvements by everyone rather than 100 per cent improvement by one person.

To see exactly how the BIP can help facilitate continuous improvement, consider the high-level process chart for the domestic appliance sales and service organization illustrated in Figure 5.11. Using this illustration let us assume that the external customer wishes to change the despatch and delivery routines currently being provided by warehousing. However, warehousing cannot accommodate this change without help. You might like to consider which other departments are likely to be affected.

It is probable that most departments will be affected in some way. But the most obvious effects are likely to be with service operations, central administration, sales, telephone bureau and purchasing and supplies. Why? Because all of these are direct component parts of the supplier/customer chain to the warehouse. Therefore, to carry out the external customer's request the warehouse manager will probably need to ask the service operations manager to modify his/her department's activities. Following this, the service operations manager will then have to request other changes from the central administration manager, and so on.

This is an example of the supplier/customer chain facilitating continuous improvement. However, where a manager genuinely cannot meet a request, this provides an ideal opportunity to set up a project team to look into the problem (this will be discussed in detail in Chapter 6).

TRAINER'S TIP

It is often little improvements which make a big difference in an organization. Your job is to help everyone to appreciate the importance of their own contribution. When people say things like, 'Yes but I'm just the cleaner', 'I just stack the shelves and load the lorries', 'I'm only the wages clerk', then you cannot afford to miss these opportunities to reinforce the importance of all of these activities.

Another illustration of change affecting the entire organization is where the chief executive sets new annual targets. Usually the targets will be cascaded down through all levels of the organization and across all functions. But in order for the cascade to be successful a number of points need to be kept in mind:

- The object of the cascade is to enable change – ie, activity will take place to achieve the target. This point is critical.
- People will work harder, more diligently and more effectively if they know that they will benefit as a result. This is important for how managers communicate new targets.
- As targets are cascaded, the language and terminology must change. Expressions like 'return on assets' or 'capital employed' may be understood in the boardroom but they become meaningless on the shopfloor. During the cascade it is important to use the listener's language.
- Progress requires ongoing monitoring – put progress charts on the wall so that everyone can see how things are changing.
- Walk the floor – managers in particular must regularly walk and talk to their people. Talking about targets is important but so is showing genuine interest and concern for the person, their environment, their feelings, ideas, family, etc.

What is the Cost of Quality?

In many organizations between 20 and 35 per cent of turnover is composed of unnecessary cost incurred by the organization. In other words, many organizations spend large sums of money simply ensuring that what goes out of the door to a customer is what is supposed to go out of the door.

To give an example of this, consider two work teams in the same factory who use identical raw materials, tools and equipment to make identical products. This is illustrated in Figure 5.21.

Team A makes and delivers the product for £100.00 whereas team B's costs are £75.00. Why the difference? Is it because team A:

- were slower and therefore the manhours cost was high?
- used more consumable items such as solder, flux, washers, etc?
- were more clumsy and needed to carry out repairs?
- missed the delivery lorry and had to send it by more expensive special delivery?
- or any number of other reasons?

This simple example illustrates that poor quality costs money. If the products are actually sold to the customer for £125.00 then clearly team B are much more profitable to the company. Furthermore, the company would be much more profitable if both teams worked to team B's standards. Managers and employees alike can all influence the cost of

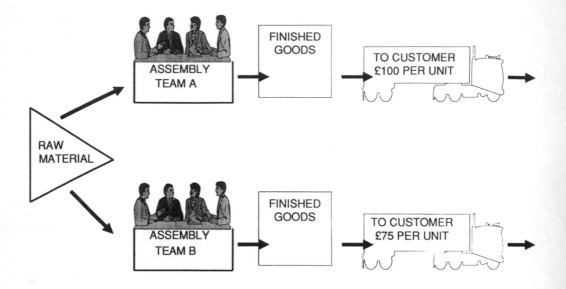

Figure 5.21 *Cost comparison*

quality and achieve continuous unit cost reduction – but it must be planned and not left to fate.

Managing the cost of quality starts by understanding how costs arise. We would favour categorizing costs under four headings.

1. Internal failure

Costs associated with activities or items used within the organization which are unnecessary and do not add value, eg:

- loss on seconds
- breakages/rejects
- consumables
- excessive stationery
- premium transportation costs
- management fire-fighting
- excessive raw material stock
- excessive work in progress
- old/discounted stock
- wasted building space
- under-utilized computer/high tech capacity
- salaries and wages for time spent on any of the above.

2. External failure

Costs associated with failure once the customer has taken receipt of the product or service, or costs incurred in persuading the customer to take receipt of the product or service, eg:

- second visit costs
- special discounts
- entertainment
- transport
- accommodation.

3. Appraisal

This could be construed as a sub-set of internal failure costs. However, this category specifically concentrates on costs associated with examination and inspection, eg:

- on-line inspection
- final examination
- raw materials inspection
- raw material testing equipment
- second checks/supervision
- customer/supplier audits.

4. Prevention

The cost of all activities or items associated with reducing or eliminating NVA, also the cost of any item or activity aimed at improvement, eg:

- quality assurance time and labour
- management training
- staff training
- operator training
- quality improvement projects
- quality bonus.

You might like to spend a few minutes thinking about costs in your organization under each of these headings. In your work with managers, it is important to allow them to identify their own cost items.

Most organizations regularly hold senior management progress/performance meetings where costs are usually a major item. With TQM organizations these conversations still take place but not just in the boardroom. Work teams also examine their quality costs and display them on a chart in a prominent position in the work area. TQM recognizes that it is here, on the shop floor, in the office, or out on the site that real cost savings can be achieved. These are the people who are in a position to affect the situation directly and immediately.

TRAINER'S TIPS

Part of your role as a trainer or consultant involves developing an awareness of TQM and encouraging accountability. Helping work teams to use the cost of quality is one of the best indicators of how you can add value to the organization.

Reluctance by managers to share information could well be an indicator that the culture of the organization is not yet ready for this level of participation. Do be aware of the significance of this and do not try to encourage them to 'have a go'. The situation may require careful handling (see chapter 7 on cultural change).

Costs of quality are most effective when the relationship between people (particularly managers) is such that both successes and difficulties in cost control can be discussed openly without fear of chastisement.

Where relationships are defensive, to advocate analysis of the cost of quality is a nonsense. People will manipulate the figures, tell half truths and play intellectual (but stupid) games of catching one another out. This results in the cost of quality being a total fabrication and of no value. Furthermore, because it is part of the TQM initiative, the TQM drive loses credibility and could become yet another 'management initiative which never got off the ground'.

TRAINER'S TIP

When facilitating the cost of quality use your consulting skills. Data collection and diagnostic activity must be such that approaches like cost of quality are implemented when the time is right: too early could prove catastrophic, too late could be a missed opportunity. If managers wish to implement cost of quality then you will need to help them understand fully the significance of their decision. Remember, your credibility is associated with the credibility of TQM.

QUESTIONS FOR THE TQM TRAINER

- How do you see your department ... as a pyramid or part of a process? How do others see your department?
- Who are your customers – do they know that?
- Who are your suppliers – do they know that?
- How is your contribution to the organization measured?
- Who measures/evaluates your performance – your boss and/or your customers?
- How will you start introducing the concept of the BIP and what help will you need?
- How will you go about getting people to 'think TQM' when this may challenge organizational and personal norms?
- How much do you know about the external customer(s) and what their order-winning criteria are?
- Who decides what is a value-adding activity for you?
- How much of your time is spent on value-adding and non-value-adding activities?
- How frequently do you meet with your customers to discuss their requirements of you and agree evaluation criteria?
- How frequently do you provide feedback to your suppliers on how well they are doing?
- What contract or agreement needs to be made in order for you to make any necessary interventions to support the development of the BIP within your organization? (This is very relevant, particularly where the norm has been for you to operate solely within a training centre running courses.)
- How would you evaluate the cost of quality within your own department?

6 Projects

▷ SUMMARY ◁

- Projects are an important method for ensuring continuous improvement by involving everyone in the business.
- Projects require substantial training activity: assisting with the setting up of quality teams and facilitating their meetings; briefing people on the purpose of projects; training and supporting project team leaders; and training group members in problem-solving techniques.
- For projects to be successful they need to be supported by a formal structure of quality teams at both company and department level.
- A project team is not a permanent group – it is brought together to work on a specific problem and is then disbanded.
- A quality improvement project follows six stages: defining the symptoms of the problem; making a project proposal; data collection, interpretation and problem analysis; submitting proposals for a solution and implementation planning; communication and training; implementation.
- Project team members will need to be trained in a number of problem-solving techniques.

What are Projects?

As we have seen, TQM is a way of managing the business to ensure continuous improvement. Quality improvement projects are a very important method for doing this. They are a method of systematically solving problems and capitalizing on opportunities in every area of the organization.

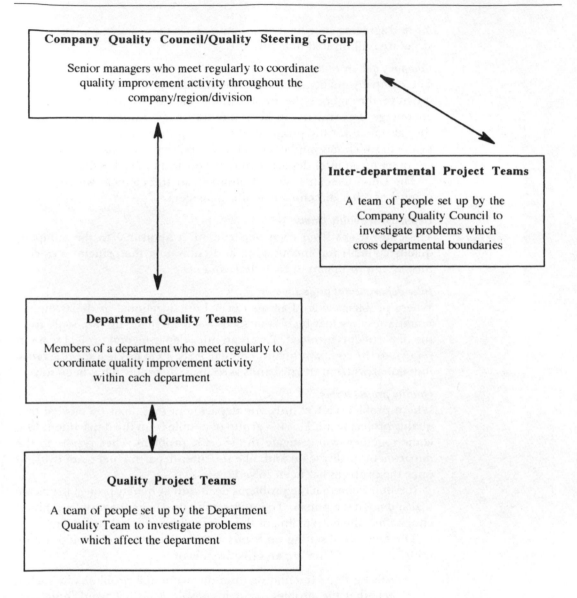

Company Quality Council/Quality Steering Group

Senior managers who meet regularly to coordinate
quality improvement activity throughout the
company/region/division

Inter-departmental Project Teams

A team of people set up by the
Company Quality Council to
investigate problems which
cross departmental boundaries

Department Quality Teams

Members of a department who meet regularly to
coordinate quality improvement activity
within each department

Quality Project Teams

A team of people set up by the Department
Quality Team to investigate problems
which affect the department

Figure 6.1 *Coordinating TQM*

If individual project groups are to be successful they need a climate in
which quality improvement is high on the agenda and a formal structure
of support. At each level of the business it is essential to have in place a
clearly defined reporting structure which is accountable for communicat-

ing and agreeing coordinated quality improvement activities. This type of structure is illustrated in Figure 6.1.

Company quality council

The company quality council is responsible for coordinating the TQM initiative throughout the organization. Part of its responsibility is to encourage departments to keep aiming for continuous improvement; they also monitor the progress of project groups. Where they identify a problem which has implications for several departments (or sites) they could set up an inter-departmental project team to tackle the issue.

The Chief Executive should always chair the council, which usually comprises other directors or senior managers.

Department quality teams

These are teams from each department (responsible to the company quality council) for encouraging and cultivating the principles of continuous improvement in each department.

Inter-departmental project teams

Where problems extend across normal organizational or departmental boundaries they may be best tackled by a team made up of people from the departments involved. This is an inter-departmental project team. It reports to the company quality council, is set up to tackle a specific cross-functional problem and disbands as soon as the problem has been solved.

Quality project teams

Where problems affect only one department these may be tackled by a quality project team. This is a group of people from the department who come together to investigate the specific problem. They report to the department quality team and, like the inter-departmental team disband once the problem has been solved.

It is important that the problems dealt with by quality project teams are real and not just cosmetic. To justify setting up a team the problem should either affect the bottom line or the needs of the external customer.

The benefits of setting up teams are considerable and should not be underestimated. They are an effective way of:

- solving departmental or inter-departmental problems in such a way that the problem remains resolved – they avoid 'quick-fix' solutions;
- tapping the creative potential of people in the organization;
- helping people feel responsible for, involved in, and committed to TQM;
- developing people – giving them an opportunity to experience team leadership and build problem-solving skills.

What is my Role during Projects?

Projects are fundamental for the success of TQM. They are a very powerful way of getting everyone in the business involved in and committed to the principles of excellence and continuous improvement. The introduction of projects as a way of life requires a great deal of change so inevitably, as a trainer, you will be at the heart of things.

As we argued in the last section, successful projects need an organizational structure to support them. Different levels of quality teams need to be set up to facilitate and drive the TQM initiative. As a trainer you will need to get involved in helping these teams to be effective, helping them clarify their role in the first place, ensuring they remain committed and perhaps facilitating their meetings.

The introduction of quality projects may also require a significant change in culture. At the very least people throughout the business will need to be briefed about the purpose of projects, how they will be constituted and what will be expected of project team members. There may be opposition to the introduction of projects. People may be hostile, suspicious or feel threatened in some way. They may need to be given a lot of time to talk through their anxieties and help with identifying the benefits to themselves.

People chosen to be members of project teams will require significant skill training. Project leaders will need skills in project management, facilitating meetings, discussion leading and problem solving. In addition members of the team will require an understanding of their role together with a range of data analysis and problem-solving techniques which may be used during the project.

You will have a supporting role during the whole process, encouraging quality teams and confronting others if they are giving insufficient support to the team. Furthermore, project team leaders may need individual help, counselling, coaching and encouragement.

TRAINER'S TIP

Remember your role in projects is to encourage and enable others to carry out projects successfully. You must be careful not to undermine what is rightfully someone else's responsibility no matter how tempting it might be. For example, if a project team is finding it difficult to make their voice heard with senior management then you should work with them to develop a strategy for making themselves heard. Above all else – don't do it for them.

What is the Structure of a Quality Improvement Project?

The objective of a quality project team is to solve a problem so that it remains solved. This requires a disciplined approach, ie, some kind of structure which guides what team members do. Whenever problems become apparent it is usually the symptoms which are spotted first and the temptation is to start thinking of immediate solutions. In our view this is the 'quick fix' which does not remove the original cause of the problem. Imposing a disciplined structure on the way a team approaches problems will help avoid this danger.

A problem-solving structure should ensure that the team:

- fully examines the symptoms that are obvious together with how they affect the business;
- identifies the causes which produce the symptoms;
- decides on a solution or course of action which will remove the cause;
- implements the solution.

To do this systematically we would adopt a six-stage approach to project development:

1. Define the symptoms of the problem.
2. Make a project proposal.
3. Collect data, interpret and analyse the problem.
4. Submit proposals for a solution and plan implementation.
5. Communicate the plan and carry out any training.
6. Implement.

Stage 1: Defining the Symptoms

The first stage is carried out by the team leader. At this point his/her main objective is to decide whether the problem is serious or important enough to justify the costs involved in further investigation. This means addressing three questions.

- *How is the customer affected by the problem?*
It is important to identify who will benefit from the problem being tackled successfully. All internal and external customers should be asked for their views at this stage.

- *How can the scale of the problem be measured?*
The purpose of quality projects is to ensure continuous improvement. Measurement is at the heart of that improvement process. If the project is to be seen to be successful then the team will need to prove that there has

been a measurable improvement. Hence, before embarking on the project the scale of the problem must be clearly measured so that a comparison can be made with the original situation once a solution has been implemented.

• *What does the problem cost?*
Costs can be measured in financial terms, time, loss of production, reduced customer satisfaction, damage to company or brand image.

TRAINER'S TIP

Many managers believe that their role involves providing answers to all questions. Consequently they could experience some difficulty working in a project team where members of staff are encouraged to solve problems. This could be a cultural difficulty – your role as a trainer is to identify such problems and help managers adopt new ways of working.

Stage 2: Making a Project Proposal

Having decided that it is worthwhile carrying out an investigation of the project, the next step is to document the evidence and obtain approval from the department quality team or company quality council. The purpose of the project proposal is to give a standard framework to the project and provide evidence that an initial investigation and assessment have already been carried out. A sample quality project proposal document is illustrated in Figure 6.2.

• *The project title*
This should be carefully chosen to indicate the general area the problem is addressing. It doesn't need to be too specific as this may pre-empt the work of the project team.

• *Source of problem*
This acts as a point of reference and should identify the person who originally raised the problem.

• *Statement of problem*
This should clearly state the nature of the problem, how it affects the customer and the costs of the problem not being resolved.

• *The objective*
This is a statement about what needs to be achieved; it will also describe the situation as it will be on successful completion of the project. It is

QUALITY PROJECT PROPOSAL

Date:	Project Title:
Source of Problem:	
Statement of problem:	
Objective:	
Means of Measurement:	
Plan of Action:	
Project Leader:	
Team Members:	

Figure 6.2 *Quality project proposal form*

important to note that on some occasions the objective might not be to remove the whole problem – this may not be cost-effective or even possible. However, any objective should be both measurable and within the grasp of the team.

* *Means of measurement*

This should contain a clear statement of how success will be measured, how it will be calculated and the method used to obtain the measurements.

- *Plan of action*

The plan should show all the steps which need to be taken to complete the project, together with an estimated completion date for each step.

- *Name of the project leader*

The name needs to be indicated. This is the person who will have overall responsibility for seeing the project through.

- *The project team*

The team needs to be very carefully chosen. The size of team needs to be the smallest number of people necessary to tackle the problem. Initially this is unlikely to be more than four, although people with specialist knowledge may be drafted in later. Team members need to be enthusiastic and committed to solving the problem; they need to have relevant knowledge of the problem and should be prepared to take responsibility for implementing the solutions. Also it is beneficial if the project team members are in some way affected by or involved in the problem.

TRAINER'S TIP

The project proposal is a critical document. It is on this information that the company quality council will either approve or stop the project. You will need to spend time with many project leaders in helping them express themselves clearly and precisely – this could have enormous training implications.

Stage 3: Data Collection, Interpretation and Problem Analysis

At this stage the team carries out thorough research to find the root causes of the problem and identifies appropriate solutions which will tackle the causes. It may not be possible to find a 100 per cent solution but the objective is to find a cost-effective strategy which will improve the situation.

Several techniques for this will be outlined in a subsequent section, but for the present we will concentrate on the overall process of the project team.

TRAINER'S TIP

This is usually the most time-consuming stage of a quality improvement project. Although it is essential that the momentum is maintained it is even more important that the analysis is thorough. Your role will include checking and monitoring that this actually happens – if necessary confronting any short cuts which individuals may wish to make.

Stage 4: Submitting Proposals for a Solution, Planning Implementation

Having identified a solution or course of action, the project leader must submit the team's proposal to either the departmental quality team or company quality council for their approval. When doing this three questions need to be considered.

- *What barriers exist to implementation?*

If the project is to be successful, inevitably there will be changes in the way things are done. This will have implications for people. Often people feel uncomfortable with change; they may feel threatened, fearful, resentful or angry when there are disruptions to the way they do their work or to their working relationships. This is especially true if they are not involved in data collection or decision-making.

The first questions to ask when planning to implement new ideas are, 'Who will be affected by these changes?' and, 'How are they likely to feel about them?' These people will need to have the changes explained to them and be given an opportunity to ask questions and express their feelings about the changes. They may also need time to come to terms with change. As a trainer your role is to get both the project leader and the team members to appreciate the importance of such considerations. If they are ignored the people affected may torpedo even the most well-meaning change.

- *What actions need to be taken to get things moving?*

An action plan needs to be agreed and carefully recorded so that everyone involved understands his/her role. The action plan should address the following questions:

- What action is to be taken?
- Why is the action to be taken?
- Who will do it?
- When will it be done?
- Where will it be done?
- How is it to be done?

- *How will the new system be maintained?*

Once the new system is in place, steps should be taken to ensure that it continues to operate effectively and becomes part of the accepted procedures. The new system will also need documenting to ensure that:

- New staff are quickly made aware of the procedure.
- The procedure continues to be followed.

- There is a recognized base from which future changes can be made.
- Similar systems can more easily be introduced elsewhere in the organization.

Stage 5: Communicating and Training

The next stage involves informing everyone who needs to know and offering appropriate training. This stage is vital. Unless it is carried out well people will not feel committed, they will not know what to do and the project will flounder. During the communicating and training stage people will need to know:

- Why the project was carried out.
- Why the changes are to be made.
- What the new system or procedure is.
- How it will affect them.
- What they need to do differently.
- What help they will get.
- When it will start.

Finally in this stage, if people need new skills they will need time to learn, practise and develop them.

TRAINER'S TIP

The project team members themselves communicate and train the people involved in any change. Your role is about making sure they have the necessary communication and training skills – once again this could have enormous training implications.

Stage 6: Implementation

A major pitfall at the implementation stage is for the team members to do everything themselves. Their role should be one of monitoring, coaching and helping others overcome any unforeseen difficulties. It may well be advisable to start implementation in a small way as a pilot. This will allow the project team the opportunity to monitor progress and ensure that their solution is actually solving the problem. When success has been achieved the project should be fully documented so that it can be used for reference if a similar problem occurs in the future.

TRAINER'S TIP

As the team members will be involved in coaching members of staff, you can provide valuable help by organizing periodic coach support group meetings.

What is the Role of the Project Team Leader?

All quality teams will require an appropriate team leader to be selected. This might be a manager or a supervisor or it could be someone with no managerial responsibilities. The important point is that the leader is familiar with the nature of the problem without being over-involved or having an axe to grind. To carry out the role he/she will need a range of problem-solving and group facilitation skills. The actual role of the leader is to:

- act as a link with the departmental quality team or company quality council;
- take responsibility for the initial investigation into the nature of the problem and distinguish between real symptoms and 'red herrings';
- manage the progress of the project;
- make practical arrangements for group meetings;
- help the team apply problem-solving techniques appropriately;
- invite technical experts to join the team if their expertise is required;
- help the team to think through ways of implementing their ideas.

In addition, the leader will need to help the team members to work together effectively. This means:

- ensuring that all group members are able to participate fully during meetings. This could involve inviting people to contribute, asking questions, and ensuring that all contributions are valued;
- helping members build on each other's ideas – effective groups stay focused on an idea and do not jump to another before discussion of the first idea is complete;
- helping the group resolve any conflict in a way which is constructive and creative;
- promoting a climate of openness where people do not feel defensive about their own involvement in the problem;
- preventing over-talking or interruptions taking place during discussions.

For team leaders to undertake this role successfully they will need a high level of self-awareness, assertiveness, sensitivity, communication and listening skills.

What Problem-solving Techniques are Available?

As we saw in the earlier section on structure, stage three of quality improvement projects includes problem analysis. This requires considerable time researching the cause of the problem, collecting data, redefining the problem and identifying possible solutions. For project teams to be successful you will need to make sure that everyone has been trained in a number of problem-solving and decision-making techniques. As a trainer this presents you with a twofold challenge: first, ensuring you understand the techniques available yourself; second, working out methods for training project team members so that they are able to apply the techniques themselves. In this section we will outline a few of the problem-solving methods available together with a few tips on how you can help others apply them.

Problem analysis can be divided into three separate activities:

- Problem identification.
- Problem definition.
- Generation of solutions.

For each activity there are a number of problem-solving techniques available.

The **problem identification** stage requires considerable thought and research into the causes of the problem. Techniques available include:

– brainstorming;
– cause and effect diagrams.

The next stage is **problem definition** where data are collected, analysed and displayed in a way which crystallizes the precise nature of the problem. Techniques available include:

– systematic data collection;
– data presentation diagrams;
– Pareto analysis.

Solution generation, as the name suggests, requires the group to examine systematically courses of action which will eradicate the causes of the problem. Techniques include:

– solution and effect diagrams.

Brainstorming

The aim of brainstorming is to generate a large number of ideas from a small group of people. Its purpose is to produce creative thought and to encourage people to look beyond the obvious. Generally it is used either at the early stages of a project to generate ideas about what the possible causes of a problem might be, or later on to assist the group identify possible solutions.

To carry out a brainstorming exercise all the members of the team need to sit together (preferably in a horseshoe so that everyone feels involved) facing a flip chart. The leader then outlines the nature of the problem and everyone in the group calls out ideas whilst the leader writes them *all* on the flip chart.

Although the success of brainstorming depends on everyone seeing it as a free-for-all, there are nevertheless certain rules which must be followed to make sure the technique is effective:

- A **leader** should be appointed for the brainstorming session. It is his/her responsibility to make sure the rules are followed. The leader need not be the project leader but it is important that it is someone who is free of any pre-formed ideas.
- **Don't evaluate**. If ideas are criticized during the ideas generation stage it will only serve to inhibit other ideas. All ideas should be recorded without comment.
- The flip chart should be **visible** to everyone and the ideas recorded so that they can be seen. If the flip chart becomes full then tear off the sheet and stick it on the wall – group members can then look back at it for further inspiration.
- Encourage **quality** throughout. It should be possible for a group to generate a lot of ideas for most problems.
- Encourage the group members to **free-wheel** and call out their ideas now matter how laughable they appear. Remember that an initially 'silly' idea may contain the seeds of something new and creative. Towards the end of a session use the 'wildest idea' technique to obtain further thoughts not previously generated. If a session ends on the wildest idea people will go away laughing and feeling they have contributed.
- Occasionally encourage the group to have a few minutes of **silent incubation**, whilst looking at the ideas listed on the chart. This can be especially helpful when ideas dry up – it often results in a flood of new ideas.
- After a brainstorming session give participants a copy of the ideas generated – if possible, allow a few days for them to '**chew them**

over' and add any further ideas which come to mind.

- Finally all of the ideas should be **evaluated**. The group needs to scrutinize all the ideas for possible winners. They might also try to convert some of the more 'way out' ideas into practical possibilities. Next they need to identify the advantages and disadvantages of each and subject each of the best ideas to 'reverse brainstorming' by asking 'In how many ways can this idea fail?'

TRAINER'S TIP

The best way for a group to learn the brainstorming technique is by doing it. Present them with a series of 'fun' problems and ask them to carry out a brainstorm on each, eg 'How many uses can you find for a paper clip?'; 'How many uses can you find for a toilet roll?' These 'silly' types of problems can be excellent for loosening up creative thinking.

Cause and Effect Diagrams

Cause and effect or fishbone diagrams are used to help a group identify and understand the underlying cause of a problem rather than the symptoms. By displaying ideas in a pictorial way it becomes easy to make sense of a lot of data while at the same time obtaining a broad picture of a problem.

The first step is for the group to brainstorm the possible causes of a problem and then categorize them under four headings:

- people;
- procedures;
- technology (including equipment and machinery);
- materials (all materials processes).

All of this information is then fed into the basic diagram. Figure 6.3 shows how a diagram can be used with an everyday example to determine the possible causes of high petrol consumption in a car.

This approach is very simple and deceptively powerful. Almost every situation at work is likely to be affected by the four basic factors – people, procedures, technology, materials. When preparing the diagram it is important that the group shows all possible causes of the problem even though most will be rejected later. When the diagram is complete the group will be able to get a very clear picture of the nature of the problem. Then, working from the information on the diagram they will be able to

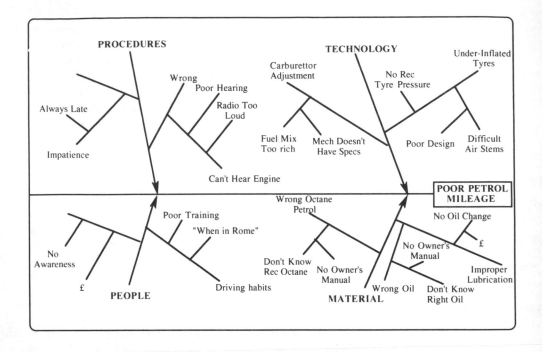

Figure 6.3 *Cause and effect diagram*

decide which specific areas to investigate. The process of assessing priorities and elimination will allow the 'root cause' of the problem to be found.

Data Collection

Having identified the possible causes of a problem through brainstorming and applying a cause and effect diagram, the group next needs to research thoroughly the most likely causes and collect as much data as possible about each cause.

The purpose of data collection is to understand thoroughly the current situation in order to be able to analyse and improve it. There are of course many different types of data available and it is possible that groups will be tempted to go on collecting more and more data eventually becoming overwhelmed. As the trainer you will need to intervene if this appears likely. Other points which the group should remember during data collection include:

- Having a definite purpose – being very clear about why they are collecting particular information.

- Relevance – it is important that the group ignores everything that is not relevant to the problem under investigation. They need to collect only one set of data at a time and keep it simple – this will avoid confusion.
- The data must be accurate and measurable. They need to be very carefully observed and recorded in terms of quantity, time, quality and/or cost.
- The data must be representative. They should accurately reflect normal conditions. For example, collecting data at times like Christmas Eve, the end of the financial year, or during a flu epidemic will probably not represent normal conditions.

Data Presentation

Having collected the data the group now needs to assemble and present them in a simple and meaningful way. Typically, if people have a choice between figures, words and pictures they are likely to find pictures the easiest to understand. It follows therefore that whenever possible groups should present their data in diagrammatic form using charts or graphs. Techniques for doing this include:

- pie charts;
- bar charts;
- histograms;
- graphs, etc.

Pareto Analysis

Pareto analysis is named after the Italian economist Vilfredo Pareto who found that 80 per cent of the wealth was in the hands of 20 per cent of the population. This 80–20 rule holds true for a great many things in life. Pareto analysis is a simple system used to differentiate the 'vital few from the trivial many' causes of a problem. In problem-solving a group can use the Pareto Principle to identify where the greater part of the problem lies. If 80 per cent of a problem arises from 20 per cent of the causes then it makes sense to tackle the 20 per cent, eliminating most of the problem.

Pareto analysis involves four steps:

1. Decide which 'causes' to collect data about
Decide the categories of the data items and the period over which data will be collected – then collect the data.

2. Tabulate the data:
Arrange the causes in descending order and tabulate the data. Causes

137

that contain only a few items can be combined and categorized as 'others' and listed at the end, eg:

CAUSE	NUMBER
A	13
B	7
C	2
D	1
Others	2
TOTAL	25

3. Calculate the percentage and cumulative percentage

To calculate the percentage, divide the number for each cause by the total and multiply by 100. To calculate the cumulative percentage, put the top figure in the new column and going down, add each new figure to the last, eg:

CAUSE	NUMBER	%	CUM%
A	13	52	52
B	7	28	80
C	2	8	88
D	1	4	92
Others	2	8	100
TOTAL	25	100	100

4. Draw a Pareto diagram

See Figure 6.4. This example highlights the fact that 80 per cent of the problem is caused by factors A and B. If these two can be eradicated then most of the problem will be solved.

Solution and Effect Diagrams

This is a similar tool to the cause and effect diagram discussed earlier. Once again it takes the form of a fishbone diagram but this time it is used when a possible solution to a problem has to be chosen. When choosing a solution it would be unwise for a group to press ahead without thinking about costs and consequences. It is important therefore for the group to brainstorm a list of negative outcomes (however improbable) and categorize these under the same headings: people, procedures, technology, materials.

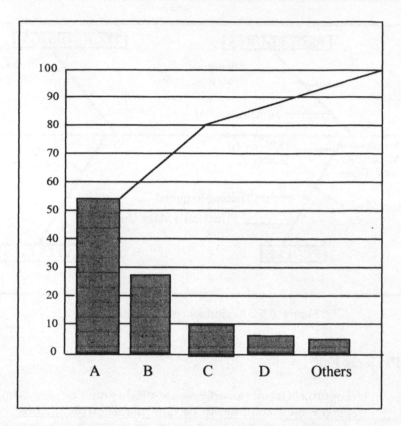

This is a special bar chart that presents information in a descending order from the largest category to the smallest. The line represents the cumulative percentage.

Figure 6.4 *Pareto diagram*

An example of a solution and effect diagram for introducing flexible working is given in Figure 6.5. The solution and effect diagram may well uncover undesirable effects that had previously escaped consideration.

As you read through this section you may have thought of other problem-solving techniques which quality teams could use – if so, please feel free to try them. Our purpose here was not to provide an exhaustive list but merely to give an overview of a few techniques which we have found of value. Having discussed quality teams, roles, structure and technique we will move on to consider why projects might fail.

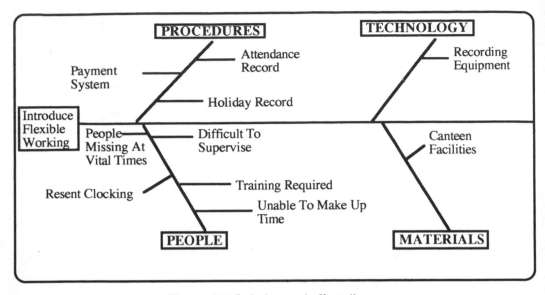

Figure 6.5 *Solution and effect diagram*

Why might Projects Fail?

For project teams to work successfully they must be seen as important and people must continue to be enthusiastic. Without these prerequisites they will quickly fail. But there are many pitfalls; they include:

- Lack of commitment by senior managers – it is essential that mangers encourage project teams, provide support and help them to implement their ideas.
- Project teams not being given significant problems – this is another aspect of low management commitment. It is essential that the problem is identified first, is recognized as being significant, and an investigatory team is set up. The alternative is to set up a project team and then look for problems.
- Project teams not being given sufficient authority or resources – it can be demotivating, for example, if a team is set up and then not given sufficient time away from the job to do the project justice.
- Lack of clarity over terms of reference – the group needs to be well briefed.
- Failure to assist in implementation. It is not sufficient simply to investigate a problem and write a report. The team needs encour-

agement to see the project through to implementation.

- Status and politics – successful project teams rely on an appropriate management style, ie, one which genuinely values people's ideas and wants to encourage their creativity.
- Lack of training – you will need to ensure that project leaders are able to facilitate the group and that all group members are trained in using the 'tools and techniques' of project management.
- Lack of coordination – project teams need to have their efforts coordinated by the departmental quality teams or company quality council. It is also useful to document and keep a register of all projects which have been completed. This can be used as a source of reference if similar problems emerge in other parts of the organization in the future (this is also part of the role of the company quality council).

QUESTIONS FOR THE TQM TRAINER

- Does your organization have in place a company quality council, departmental/regional or divisional quality teams?
- Do the quality teams focus on long-term quality issues or on day-to-day problems?
- What resistance might there be to the introduction of projects?
- How much support do project teams get from senior managers?
- How can I ensure that project teams are given significant problems to deal with?
- How can project teams be encouraged to implement their ideas?
- How can the success of projects be measured in terms of cost savings, increased profit or increased customer satisfaction?
- Are projects well coordinated by the company quality council?
- Is the team leader the most appropriate person to fulfil that role?
- Do team leaders have the necessary skills?
- How can I check that team leaders understand the structure of quality improvement projects?
- How can I help team leaders define the symptoms of problems and make project proposals?
- How can I ensure project team members have knowledge and skill in problem analysis and problem-solving techniques?

7 Management Style and Culture Change

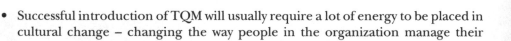

SUMMARY

- Successful introduction of TQM will usually require a lot of energy to be placed in cultural change – changing the way people in the organization manage their relationships with each other.
- Senior managers need a clear picture of how they need people to behave in a TQM organization and the implications of this for the management style.
- Personal change workshops are a way of helping people understand the culture of the organization and how it helps and hinders TQM. It also gives people a higher level of self-awareness and insight into ways of increasing personal effectiveness.

Why is Cultural Change Important in TQM?

The real key to the success of TQM is people. If the people in the business, at every level, are not committed to producing a quality product or service, then your TQM initiative is doomed to failure. It is relatively easy to change technology, systems and procedures. It is much more difficult to change people's attitudes to work, their perceptions of management, their values, their motivation and their behaviour. Yet this is exactly the challenge confronting you if your company is committed to TQM.

The culture existing in many organizations is simply not conducive to the achievement of excellence. We have worked in many organizations where people recognize that the culture in which they work is one of: 'covering our backs'; 'finding someone to blame'; 'lack of trust'; 'people being kept in the dark'; 'us and them'; 'nobody listening'.

TRAINER'S TIP

If you want to get a picture of the culture in your organization ask groups at all levels to answer the following questions:
To make this a better place to work:

- What should we all do less of?
- What should we all do more of?
- What should we continue to do the same?

A tabulation of all the answers will give you a pretty good idea of the culture of the business.

Changing such a culture to one in which people work together collaboratively takes a lot of energy, commitment and time. For this reason this is the part of the TQM jigsaw that is often neglected. As a TQM trainer, however, this is your primary responsibility: to confront people at all levels of the business with the negative results of their own behaviour and get their commitment to changing behaviour. So how do you do this?

When we work with an organization which is at the early stages of TQM and just beginning to examine the implications of their present management style and organizational culture, we ask the board or senior management team to think quite deeply about three questions:

- What is a TQM employee? How does this description differ from the way our employees behave now?
- What is a TQM manager? How does this differ from the way our managers behave now?
- What are the implications for the board?

These are questions we'd like to help you consider in the next three sections of this chapter.

What is a TQM Person?

Of course there is no such thing as a TQM person. All people are different and TQM organizations are not full of clones of a certain kind; quite the contrary. However, TQM does require people to have a commitment to quality and to the company, and their behaviour needs to reflect this. Generally speaking, people will do what they are rewarded for doing. So, when embarking on TQM the senior management team needs to clarify their picture of how people will behave in their TQM organization. If they compare this ideal with how people actually operate now, this will help them develop a strategy for culture change.

TRAINER'S TIP

Ask your senior management team to list what they think are the characteristics of a TQM person. It will help focus their thinking if they compile their list under the following headings:

- The way he/she does the job
- Social skills
- Attitudes
- Self-esteem

When they have produced a comprehensive list give them a copy of Appendix 1 (at the end of this book) and ask them to agree a rating for people currently in the organization.

What is a TQM Manager?

If your business needs people who are committed to quality and to the company then there are likely to be profound implications for the way they are managed. TQM requires a very different management style from that which has been traditional in many organizations. Traditional management has placed a great deal of emphasis on controlling people. This is evidenced in the importance placed on piecework, clocking in, close supervision, etc. TQM, however, places the emphasis on empowering people, helping them build the skills, confidence and attitudes to take responsibility for their own work, rather than forcing them to do it.

Before going on we would like you to take a sheet of paper and list the skills, attitudes and knowledge required of managers if they are to develop and successfully manage TQM people. When you have done that look at our profile of a Total Quality manager in Appendix 2 at the end of this book. Here we have tried to compare the characteristics of managers who adopt a 'traditional' management style with those of a TQM management style.

TRAINER'S TIP

When using the instrument 'The Characteristics of TQM Management Style' with a group of managers you can promote maximum thought and discussion if you follow these steps:

1. Give them the handout which lists the characteristics of a traditional management style (left hand column only). Ask the group to identify the corresponding characteristics of a TQM management style.
2. Give them our list of characteristics of a TQM management style to compare with theirs.
3. Against each characteristic ask them to agree a description of the predominant management style in your organization.

How do I go about Influencing the Culture?

Cultural change is a very complex business which requires a lot of commitment, a lot of patience and a desire to succeed. However, without a thorough examination of the management style and the culture of the business, TQM is likely to be doomed to failure.

The culture of an organization is all the interactions which take place between people. It is about how people work together, their relationships and the feelings engendered by their behaviour. The culture of an organization includes:

- management style
- who makes decisions and how
- communications; one-way or two-way
- who participates in decision-making
- status
- perceived power or powerlessness
- whether people feel listened to
- how people react to new ideas – constructively or destructively
- opportunities for individual development and growth
- the degree of support, openness and trust
- the amount of feedback people give to each other
- how conflict is handled; constructively or destructively
- whether people compete with each other or work collaboratively
- how problems about gender, race and disability are handled
- the way feelings are handled

- involvement
- commitment
- motivation

Many organizational problems are to do with culture, how people behave and feel. Yet very few organizations really attempt to deal with these issues. This is probably because they are very difficult to quantify and impossible to control. Yet if you are seeking excellence in your business it is vital that you promote an organizational culture which facilitates excellence. Thus an essential component of TQM is the introduction of personal change programmes which help everyone in the organization – directors, managers and employees – to work on elements of the culture which work against business success and the vision.

TRAINER'S TIP

A good way of introducing a group to the importance of cultural issues in the organization is to ask each person individually to answer the following questions:
- What are the things my team does well?
- What are the things I enjoy and find satisfying about working in this business, (department, team)?
- What are the things my team does less well?
- What are the things I least enjoy and find frustrating about working here?

When everyone has answered the questions ask them to call out their answers. Log them on a flip chart by grouping together factors which relate to tasks and activities, those which relate to systems and procedures and those which relate to culture.

What does Personal Change Training Involve?

Personal Change Workshops should be designed to help people examine the way they behave in the organization both as groups and as individuals. A successful Personal Change Workshop will enable participants to increase their understanding of the culture of the organization and how cultural issues help or hinder business effectiveness. In addition they will need to have increased their own self-awareness, looked at how they themselves manage working relationships and their strengths and weaknesses. Obviously personal and group action planning are important aspects of personal change training.

The objectives of a personal change workshop should include:

- Helping managers to gain an insight into their own management and personal styles, and to identify a range of other styles that may be appropriate.

- Improving people's awareness and understanding of the style of their organization and to develop action plans to facilitate change within the business (in terms of leadership style and teamwork).
- Participants receiving and also being encouraged to give constructive feedback to others on their behaviour, and giving suggestions as to ways they may change and the potential benefits of doing so.
- Development of personal action plans which involve talking with their boss and other members of their team about managerial issues raised in the programme and what needs to be done in the business.
- Practising a range of 'people contact skills' which will help them to be more visible and skilful in handling relations in the team, with suppliers and customers and improve their overall effectiveness.

Such programmes require a high degree of flexibility. It is important to help managers work on their own issues rather than staying rigidly married to a predetermined training programme.

TRAINER'S TIP

At the beginning of a personal change workshop it is important to establish a 'learning contract' with each member of the group. To do this ask each group member to answer the following questions, write their answers on a flip chart and put the flip chart on the wall:.

- What are my personal objectives for this workshop?
- What do I need to do during the workshop if I'm to achieve these objectives?
- What help do I need from other people?
- What might I do which will sabotage my own learning?

These contracts will help you structure the programme in a way that genuinely meets the needs of the group.

Getting people to change their behaviour is notoriously difficult. The training world is littered with examples of people attending wonderful courses, leaving full of enthusiasm and then being unable to implement their learning on returning to work. Personal change should be seen as much more than a training course.

If you are going to use personal change workshops to influence the culture and really change behaviour they need to take place within an organizational framework. You need to carefully plan:

- how you will prepare people before the workshop;
- how to ensure that the workshop itself has maximum impact on the participants;
- how people will receive follow-up and support after the workshop when they implement new skills and try new styles of behaviour back at work.

Before the Workshop

If off-the-job training is to be successful, a great deal of preparation and planning is necessary prior to the programme. The first thing to consider is the make-up of each group. Often it is best done in working teams so that the issues most important to each team can be tackled. On other occasions it may be important to mix people from a number of departments where issues concerning customer/supplier relationships are to be discussed. Sometimes you may consider that it is important that people from a variety of levels in the organization are represented. The key factor here is that the mix of people should reflect the key issues to be worked on.

Each individual attending the workshop should be well briefed by his or her manager as well as the trainer who will be running the workshop. The participant needs to know why he or she is being asked to attend, the purpose of the workshop and what they are expected to achieve. This is a good opportunity for the individual to receive feedback from the manager. The manager should also explain what kind of support will be available when the participant returns to work. Finally, the participants may need time to talk through their own feelings and any fears or concerns they have about attending the programme. It is essential that no one feels they have been forced to attend the workshop.

The Workshop

Successful training programmes are essential if real cultural change is to take place. You will need to use a number of behavioural models which will help people better understand the organizational culture and their own behaviour. (We will say more about these models in the next section.) However, you must avoid being seen as over-theoretical. The models you use should be simple and easily taken on board. You need to ensure that they really do help participants make sense of their own experience in the organization. They should also help people identify alternative ways of behaving.

It is vital that during the workshop you model the behaviour you wish people to adopt throughout the business. If the vision includes an open trusting climate where people are honest with each other then you need to encourage such a climate during the workshop. This means that there needs to be lots of opportunities for people to practise new skills and behaviour.

Perhaps most difficult of all, you should resist the temptation to collude with your groups. Groups often collude with each other to pretend that things are much better than they are. They deny that there are any real cultural problems; they will be adamant that they adopt a participative management style when the reality is very different. If you see this happening you need to be prepared to confront the inconsistencies between how people say they behave and their actual behaviour as you see it.

Throughout the workshop you should encourage people to write action plans. These can be agreed by groups, departments or individuals. When they leave the programme they should have a clear idea of what they need to do as a group or team to contribute to the cultural change the company is working towards. They also need to have a clear strategy for developing their own individual skills and effectiveness. Encourage them to make these plans as concrete as possible. They should include success criteria, time scales and sources of support. They should be clear about the specific people with whom they need to build more effective working relationships.

After the Programme

Skill loss starts immediately, so it is vital that each person is encouraged to implement their action plans as soon as they return to work. They need to be supported while they try out new behaviours and rewarded for any success. At an individual level there needs to be de-briefing sessions with each manager. As a trainer you may be able to offer support during the de-briefing.

Beware, though, of usurping the role of the manager. At a group level, it can be very helpful to set up support groups where people can discuss their progress and compare successes and failures. We often find that people from the same department who have attended personal change programmes separately need time to come together to discuss the implications of their experience of the programme for the way they work together in the department.

How do I Use Behavioural Models to Facilitate Cultural Change?

Over the past 50 years behavioural scientists have developed a multitude of models and theories designed to help us better understand individual and organizational behaviour. As a TQM trainer you need to have a range of such models which you can use to cast light on organizational issues as they arise.

When choosing such models we apply a number of criteria. First, they must be seen as relevant to the issue which has been identified by a group or an individual as being an important problem, and to their situation. Second, the theory should be simple and easily understood. A theory that takes more than 20 minutes to explain and understand is probably too complicated. Finally, the theory should help your clients clarify the problem they have identified, and help them work on alternative strategies for dealing with the problem.

TRAINER'S TIP

When using behavioural theories try to follow these seven phases:

1. DIAGNOSIS – make sure you have clarified the organizational issue to be worked on and got the group's commitment to working on it. Define the problem in their words not yours.
2. CHOOSE THE THEORY – make sure it is relevant to the problem that has been diagnosed.
3. EXPLORE CURRENT BEHAVIOUR – ask group members to give examples of how they or others handle the problem now. They should do this in their own words. Describe the situations in as much detail as possible, including their own feelings and reactions.
4. INTRODUCE THE THEORY – by doing so at this stage you can immediately relate it to the examples given in Phase 3. Help group members to re-explore their examples in the light of the theory.
5. RELATE THE THEORY TO THE ORGANIZATION – ask the group to describe the organization or the specific problem in terms of the theory.
6. RELATE THE THEORY TO THE INDIVIDUAL – Help individuals identify their own preferred styles of behaving in terms of the theory. This can be done by:
   - asking them to select what they feel is their most preferred and least preferred style of behaving;
   - using pencil and paper instruments;
   - asking them to give each other feedback on what they see as each other's most preferred style of behaviour.
7. ACTION PLANNING – help the group clarify ways in which they can operate more effectively in the future, either collectively or individually.

What Behavioural Theories and Models are Available and How do I Find Them?

Many behavioural theories, models and instruments are available. Most of them can help people examine their own style of behaviour and also gain an insight into how the whole organization works. Some are simply descriptions of the theory, others use questionnaires and instruments which produce a profile for each person. Some models which we find useful when running personal change programmes include:

Situational Leadership	By P Hersey and K Blanchard, Pfeiffer & Co
Situational Leadership II	Blanchard Training
The New Managerial Grid	By R Blake and J Mouton, Gulf Publishing
Thomas Kilmann Conflict Mode Instrument	Available from Xicom Inc.
ASSERTION THEORY	Many books now available. These include:
The Right To Be You	Nancy Paul, Chartwell Bratt
Assertion Training, a Facilitator's Guide	Collen Kelley, Pfeiffer & Co.
I'm OK – You're OK	T Harris, Pan
A Guide to Transactional Analysis	D Barber, Gower Press
Personal Style Inventory	Hogan and Champagne, Organization Design & Development Inc.
Explorations in Managing	A Zoll, Adison Wesley. Combines many useful exercises and instruments on management style, decision-making, effective thinking, motivation, etc.
Developing Human Resources Annuals	Pfeiffer & Co. Contains a range of instruments and exercises useful for personal and individual development.

QUESTIONS FOR THE TQM TRAINER

- Do senior managers have a vision of the kind of people a TQM business requires?
- Do senior managers have a vision of the style of management the business will require? Are they clear about the changes they themselves will need to make?
- Do you have a clear idea of the elements which make up the culture of the organization?
- Have you got commitment for a programme of personal change from the top?
- Is the senior management team prepared to attend a personal change workshop?
- Are members of the senior management team prepared to get involved in supporting your running personal change workshops for middle managers?
- Are people attending personal change workshops sufficiently well briefed?
- Do you have a range of behavioural theories, instruments and exercises which will help people understand their own and others' behaviour in the organization?
- Do people leave personal change workshops with personal and group action plans to which they are committed?
- Is there a system for supporting individuals and groups during this period of cultural change?

8   Communication

▷   SUMMARY   ◁

- Communication is fundamental to the success of TQM. Everyone in the organization requires a high level of communication skills.
- It is important to regularly audit the communication process to identify where barriers exist.
- Often the root causes of communication difficulties between individuals or departments lie in the culture of the organization. Trainers need to be able to help groups examine and confront these issues.
- There is a wide range of communication media available. These not only transmit information but can also convey subtle messages about the management style of the organization.

What are the Implications of TQM for Communication in the Business?

The success of any human enterprise depends on how effectively people communicate with each other. Wars have been lost, business opportunities wasted and relationships soured simply because people have failed to communicate. Over the years a great deal of thought, time, energy and money has been directed towards the problem of improving communication in organizations. Yet 'poor communication' is still blamed for all kinds of organizational ills. This is probably because the words 'poor communication' are so general and cover a whole array of more specific problems. Before reading on you may wish to write down what the words 'poor communication' mean for you.

We spend much of our time helping organizations work on problems which are often presented in the first place as 'communication problems'. The first thing we try to do is help our clients to be more specific about the symptoms and nature of the problem, and so make it more manageable. For example, how to:

- improve the effectiveness of meetings;
- improve the quality of information passed between departments;
- improve the quality of information passed up and down the organization;
- prevent dysfunctional conflict between departments;
- eradicate distrust between employees, supervisors and managers;
- ensure that all employees are kept up-to-date with important matters to do with the business;
- help everyone in the business be more open with each other;
- confront difficulties which team members have in working with each other;
- overcome the difficulties inherent in having people in the business spread across the country or even the world;
- ensure that people in the business feel listened to.

The list is endless. Suffice to say that communication must be addressed by your TQM initiative.

TRAINER'S TIP

Don't let anyone in your organization get away with describing a problem in very vague and over-generalized terms like, 'it's a communication problem'. Ask them to be more specific, give examples, say how the problem manifests itself. Try to get them to quantify the problem and describe how it affects them. Try to get them to re-define the problem in as specific terms as possible. Then, with your help, they will be better able to start to deal with the problem.

In Chapter 6 we saw that a primary prerequisite of successful TQM is empowering people in the business. The way senior and middle managers communicate plays a huge part in how committed people are to the ethos of TQM. As a trainer your role is to help all employees to take responsibility for managing relationships with their internal and external customers and suppliers. They are expected to identify and solve problems together in a collaborative way. This implies that people at all levels of the business will require a very high level of communication skills.

TRAINER'S TIP

It is important to ensure that communication skills training is not limited to managers and supervisors. You need to ensure that everyone in the organization is given an opportunity to develop a range of these skills.

So what are the implications for communication of adopting TQM and a TQM management style? With TQM, communication becomes much more than an information-passing exercise. In a traditional organization people need to be informed of decisions which affect them. In a TQM business people need timely, accurate information in order to make decisions which affect the quality of their work. They also need the support of a communication network which will enable them to communicate those decisions to others.

Getting TQM started requires people to understand:

- what TQM is about;
- how it affects them;
- what the vision is;
- what it will mean for them.

In addition, everyone in the business needs to know:

- the direction of the business;
- what decisions are being made at senior levels;
- the reason for those decisions;
- how they will be affected personally.

Communicating all of this is an ongoing process – it is a message which needs permanent reinforcement.

Managers must also encourage everyone to develop new ideas and solve problems for themselves. Success in any business is dependent on innovation; the more new ideas that are available, the more likely the business is to improve. If this is to happen, people need to feel that their ideas and views are being valued and that they are actually involved in making decisions. In short, they must feel that they are being listened to and heard.

TRAINER'S TIP

It is tempting to see communication as an exercise in transmitting information effectively, and therefore to see communication training as helping people to do better at transmitting and delivering their ideas eg effective presentation skills, influencing skills, assertiveness. These are valuable skills but you need to put 'listening skills' on the agenda. There are many exercises available to help people examine their own listening barriers and work on ways of improving their listening effectiveness.

Communication in a TQM business needs to be open, with the emphasis on honest discussion of problems and ways they can be solved, rather than 'covering your back' or looking for someone else to blame.

What is the Trainer's Responsibility for Communication?

Communication effectiveness needs to be high on the agenda of any business. So who is responsible for communication? There are several answers to this question. The ultimate accountability for communication lies with the chief executive. The style adopted in the boardroom will be reflected in the rest of the organization. If the chief executive is not committed to open communication in word and deed, then it will not materialize.

Another answer is that everybody is responsible for their part of the communication network, for ensuring there is a constructive ongoing dialogue with their customers and suppliers. This discussion between customer and supplier should include an agreement not only on the standards required but also on how the people involved will communicate. This might include:

- what information each requires of the other;
- how quickly they need that information;
- how often they will meet to discuss more general issues;
- how they wish to work together on joint problems;
- how they will handle situations where the customer's requirements change, perhaps at short notice;
- how they will handle situations where the supplier is unable to meet any of the required standards.

The trainer's role is central to the whole communication process. As a trainer you have a number of separate but overlapping roles. These are:

- auditing the communication process in the organization, identifying communication barriers and bringing them to the attention of the managers and employees involved;
- helping to break down communication problems. This involves helping people in the business to examine the reasons why they have difficulty communicating with each other, in teams, between teams and up and down the organization. It also involves working with them to overcome these barriers;
- helping people to build effective communication skills;
- helping to ensure that appropriate communication media are used;
- to act as the conscience of the business, confronting and cajoling people to follow best communication practice.

Confronting skills were examined in Chapter 2. The other four issues will be dealt with later in this chapter.

How do I Carry Out a Communication Audit?

Before carrying out a communication audit you need to ask yourself, 'Why do people need to communicate in a TQM business?' We would identify five major reasons why managers and employees need to be effective communicators. These are to ensure that:

- everyone is aware of the vision, the values of the company and its long-term goals;
- everyone understands the purpose of his/her job, where it fits in with the rest of the business and has sufficient information to do their job effectively;
- everyone is able to participate in decision-making;
- each person is able to establish an effective dialogue with his/her customers and suppliers;
- an appropriate management style is supported and maintained.

To audit communication in your business you need to carry out a survey of people at all levels and in all departments. It is useful to ask questions which explore each area of communication. One way of doing this is to design a questionnaire to be completed by everyone. An example is given in Appendix 3 at the end of this book.

How do I Help Break Down Communication Barriers?

Communication difficulties are often merely symptoms of deeper underlying problems. They can lie in any of three areas each of which will be examined in some detail – the goals and standards of performance; communications systems; and culture.

Goals and Standards of Performance

When business goals are not explicit and well communicated, people will work to different priorities. This will lead to tension, mistrust and inevitably to communication breakdown. Similarly, if the objectives of each region, department or section are not aligned, tensions will result. When TQM is working effectively these goals will be clear. However, the world is never ideal and it is important to help your clients and client departments clarify what they believe to be:

- the objectives of the business;
- their joint contribution to the objectives;
- each individual's input.

The root of what they perceive as a 'communication problem' is often a lack of clear, agreed objectives, or people working to different agendas.

TRAINER'S TIP

When working with a management project or a cross-functional team, ask each individual member to define the purpose of the team in writing, then present them, anonymously, to the whole team. Having done this ask them to identify the differences and inconsistencies between their answers, together with implications for how they work together.

Communications Systems

All organizations need a set of systems for ensuring that information reaches the people who need it. Communication difficulties might simply be the result of inadequate procedures. When investigating and working on communication problems you need to check the efficiency of the systems:

- Are there clear procedures for upwards and downwards communication, eg, briefing groups; grievance procedures; attitude surveys?
- Are there clear procedures for lateral communication, eg, regular

customer/supplier meetings; inter-department meetings; project meetings?
- Are there adequate communication media, eg, telephones, electronic mail, fax machines, notice boards – and are they used efficiently?

Culture

Very often the real cause of communication difficulties will lie in the human dimension of the organization. These difficulties may be inherent in the way people manage relationships with each other, within teams, between teams or departments, and between the various levels of management. As a trainer you may be asked to facilitate meetings between members of a team, between members of different departments, between various levels of management or between suppliers and customers. If the stated purpose of such a meeting is to sort out communication difficulties, you would be well advised to look at the problem more deeply and help the group explore how they manage their working relationships.

Major causes of communication breakdown include:

- badly handled conflict;
- inter-departmental competition and rivalry;
- hierarchy and status;
- inappropriate management style;
- lack of openness and trust;
- prejudice and personal dislike;
- distorted perceptions of each other.

Where such problems exist your role is to help the group identify, acknowledge and talk about them in a constructive manner. This will involve your using high levels of active listening, diagnostic questioning and confronting.

TRAINER'S TIP

When working with inter-departmental or inter-disciplinary groups ask each group to work in a separate room to draw a picture of how they see each of the other groups. They should also draw a picture of themselves as they think the others see them.

Bring all the groups together, put all the pictures on the wall and ask each group to describe what they have drawn. The result can be quite revealing.

What Communication Skills do People Need?

In a TQM organization the role of a manager is different from that in a traditional organization. He or she will require skills in facilitating groups and meetings, counselling, coaching, training, giving feedback, supporting, confronting and leading discussions, among many others. Non-managers will need skills in clarifying customers' needs, ensuring suppliers know what is required, handling conflict and collaborative problem-solving.

You will need, then, to carry out a lot of training, at all levels of the organization. We would suggest that your training includes opportunities for everyone to enhance their facility with the following skills:

- presenting facts, ideas, opinions and feelings clearly to individuals and groups;
- listening and clarifying what other people are trying to say so that you really understand them;
- asking questions which ensure you get the information you need;
- checking out and dealing with people's feelings – a lot of communication problems are actually to do with how people feel;
- giving feedback on people's performance and behaviour in a way that is helpful to them;
- differentiating between facts, opinions, feelings and assumptions which often get confused in everyday language and can lead to a lot of communication difficulties;
- writing in a way that is unambiguous and easy to understand.

In Chapter 4 we outlined a model of experiential learning. These communication skills are ones that can only be learned experientially. When running training events in these areas you should structure a series of exercises which help people to really explore and experience each skill and reflect on ways they can improve their own effectiveness.

What Media are Available?

The media used to transmit and receive information need to be both appropriate and well used. As a TQM trainer part of your job may well be to advise on the appropriateness of various communication media, to train people in their use and to ensure that the various media continue to be used appropriately.

When measuring the effectiveness of any medium, four questions need to be asked:

- Is it an appropriate vehicle for passing on information?
- Are people using it correctly?
- What unconscious or implicit messages is it giving?
- Is it moving the business closer to the vision?

The actual media available for communication in the organization are relatively limited. They include:

- face-to-face meetings with individuals and groups;
- team briefings;
- performance and progress charts;
- notice boards;
- suggestion schemes;
- videos;
- the tannoy or public address system;
- internal memos, reports and discussion documents;
- computer databases;
- electronic mail;
- telephones and fax machines.

All these media have advantages and disadvantages and each helps to facilitate the communication process in a different way. It is vital that the organization has an appropriate mix of communication media.

A good measure of the mix of communication media being used is to ask whether they generally facilitate one-way or two-way communication. Are they simply vehicles for senior managers to pass information down the organization or are they designed to encourage people to generate their own ideas, express their feelings and opinions, and have them listened to? A communication system which encourages dialogue between people in all departments and at all levels of the business is more likely to encompass a TQM ethos than one which simply passes down edicts from the top.

You might also ask questions about the information itself. Is it honest? How much is hidden behind the excuse of confidentiality. Is it consultative or authoritarian in tone? What channels are there for expressing ideas, opinions and feelings? All of these questions will help you clarify whether the communication media being used in the organization are moving you closer to or further from the vision.

It is important to remember that many aspects of the working environment communicate an unconscious message about the degree to which people are valued. When people have different terms and conditions of employment, different restaurants, different hours of work, this can indicate that some people are valued more than others. Even the seating arrangements in an office can indicate that people are trusted or not trusted.

TRAINER'S TIP

Whenever you receive a memo, read a notice board or attend a meeting, ask yourself 'How does this piece of communication make me feel? Does it enhance or diminish my feelings of self-worth? Does it convey that I am an important member of the organization or someone of little importance?' Your own feelings will tell you a lot about the unconscious messages being conveyed by the communication media in the organization.

Performance Charts

The purpose of any work team is to supply their internal and external customers with what they have asked for to the standards they require. It is important that they always focus on their customers' requirements and standards and encourage work groups to produce related performance charts. Indeed a significant feature of TQM organizations is the display of these performance measures.

These displays need to be visible and colourful, as well as simple to read. It is important that they are owned by the work group. They should update them themselves rather than depend on the manager to do this. Above all the measures used should be those which are asked for by the customer, not ones chosen by the work group.

TRAINER'S TIP

When visiting departments ask people about their measures of performance and how they display them. Always ask how often their customers require the information they display. If they are not clear about this, you should be able to help them to identify measures which are really important to their customers.

QUESTIONS FOR THE TQM TRAINER

- Have you carried out a communication audit of each part of the organization? If so, what priorities did it highlight?
- Do you have sufficient facilitating skills to help groups and departments examine and confront the root causes of what are initially identified as 'communication problems'?
- Do you have available a range of experiential exercises which you can use to help people build and develop the range of communication skills they need?
- What unconscious messages are transmitted by the communication media in the organization?
- Is there an effective system of briefing groups?
- Do teams display and update their performance measures and how they are performing against them?
- Are these performance measures really the ones required by the internal or external customer?
- Are notice boards used appropriately?
- Do people feel they receive the information they need?

9 Epilogue

We have now reached the end of our tour through TQM. Hopefully you will have realized that it involves much more than tinkering with the fringes of how an organization operates. TQM means profound re-examination and restructuring at all levels. For some companies this may prove to be a monumental challenge, whereas for others the transition may be much more gentle. However, we believe it is one which is essential for corporate survival and growth through the rest of this decade. As you worked your way through the text we also hope that you will have gained a much better understanding of the implications of TQM for both you and your customers and how you can contribute towards TQM implementation.

Can we end by emphasizing once again that as a trainer your role is unique – in a sense you contribute nothing. How your customers choose to tackle and implement TQM is their responsibility. However, they are unlikely to be able to do it successfully without your help. In this respect your role is an organizational equivalent of a catalyst in a chemical reaction. Without the presence of the catalyst the reaction is unlikely to take place (or will only happen very slowly). Once the catalyst is introduced then change proceeds rapidly. This is your main contribution towards TQM – catalysing improvement and change at every opportunity. This may be very different to your role in the past, but the rewards are immense. Perhaps for the first time training will be seen as the vital agent of change in all organizations – the choice is yours. For our part we close by wishing you every success.

Appendix 1 Characteristics of TQM People

Below, on the left, is a list of characteristics which have been identified by managers in several organizations as being some of those ideally possessed by people working in a TQM business. On the right is a description of the opposite characteristic. For each item decide where you would put people at present working in your organization, then write your reason for each rating.

| Very clear about needs of external/internal customers | 5 | 4 | 3 | 2 | 1 | Not conscious of either external or internal customers |

Reason

| Able to make significant decisions which affect quality | 5 | 4 | 3 | 2 | 1 | Tightly controlled by supervisors, the systems or technology |

Reason

| Understands the goals of the business | 5 | 4 | 3 | 2 | 1 | No understanding of business goals |

Reason

| Highly trained | 5 | 4 | 3 | 2 | 1 | Little training |

Reason

High level of communication skills	5	4	3	2	1	Low level of communication skills

Reason

Says 'we'	5	4	3	2	1	Says 'them' and 'us'

Reason

Able to express needs to internal suppliers	5	4	3	2	1	Little or no direct communication with internal suppliers

Reason

Able to develop good relationships with internal and external customers	5	4	3	2	1	Little or no direct contact with internal or external customers

Reason

Quality conscious	5	4	3	2	1	Disregards quality

Reason

Self-starting and self-controlling	5	4	3	2	1	Needs close supervision

Reason

Expects to be involved in decision-making	5	4	3	2	1	Expects 'management' to make all decisions

Reason

Assertive	5	4	3	2	1	Non-assertive or aggressive

Reason

Proud of producing quality work	5	4	3	2	1	Indifferent to quality of work

Reason

Feels valued by the company	5	4	3	2	1	Feels undervalued by the company

Reason

Appendix 2
Characteristics of TQM
Management Style

Listed here are the styles and behaviours we believe characterize the TQM manager, along with the traditional style. It is likely that you may disagree with some of the words used; that's OK.

Traditional Management Style	TQM Management Style
Being Customer-centred	
The role of the customer The customer is obviously important as he pays our wages. However, often we know best and it is therefore in his own interest to let us get on with production and leave us alone.	**Total customer focus** We exist to serve the customer; without him we are nothing. It is essential that everyone in our organization believes this message and lives this message.
Customer satisfaction Our customers are also loyal and trusted friends. They've been with us for years. We'll be alright.	**Continuous improvement for the customer** We need to continually improve everything we do in order to consistently satisfy our customers.
Quality We know when we've done a good job.	**Customer-perceived quality** Meeting the needs of the customer takes precedence. If the customer says it's poor quality, it is poor quality. If the customer says it's excellent, then it's good but we can do it better.
Who is the customer? The person who buys our product.	**Who is the customer?** We have many customers. Certainly the people who buy our products are

customers but so are our employees. Everyone in the production process is a customer of the previous person (supplier). All our customers have the same rights to expect quality in everything we do.

Work Priorities
Maintaining high levels of production, keeping the system working and many others.

Quality must always be the first priority
No explanation required.

Our Employees

They are subordinates

They work for me

They are people

We all work together
For the company, ourselves and each other.

Focus on the task
Our subordinates are 'the means to an end'. It is unfortunate, but without them we will achieve nothing.

Concentrate on the people
It is the people who make the system work. It is the people who work the process. Without them we are nothing. It is the people that make the difference!

Shared culture
Never mind culture, we have targets and objectives to be achieved.

Shared culture
A healthy shared quality culture is essential to achieving excellent performance. We need to develop and constantly work at maintaining a quality culture so that everyone habitually strives for and achieves total quality in everything they do.

Involving people
The average human being dislikes work and will do everything possible to avoid getting involved.

Involving people
We all need to genuinely believe in the value of all our people and desire their involvement as everyone has imagination, ingenuity and creativity just waiting to be used.

Change
We've always done it this way. It's worked for us in the past and I see no reason to change it now.

Change
It is essential that we have an expectation of change, and encourage others to share this expectation.

Feedback
I give the feedback around here. If you hear nothing then everything must be OK but, don't worry, I'll let you know when you get it wrong!

Working to benefit others
What can my subordinates give me and the department?

What can I get out of them?

Management philosophy
People are basically lazy, irresponsible, avoid responsibilities, need direction and lack ambition. The only solution is to be authoritarian.

Instruct on managerial requirements
Send a memo. Put it on the board. On occasions (once or twice a year) tell people what you require of them.

'I'll be in my office'
Manager spends a lot of time in the office – a bit remote.

Be the boss
Controls others. Tells people what to do. Wants to be 'in charge'. Unconcerned

Feedback
It is essential that we create an environment (by doing) in which everyone welcomes and encourages feedback on their performance and how it affects others. (The king has no clothes on.)

Working to benefit others (adding value)
I need to make other people feel important, therefore how I behave, the words I use, the gestures I make are very influential. 'What can I do today which can help others achieve?'

Leadership
People have different needs in different circumstances therefore leadership should be determined by the particular situations.

Articulate the TQM philosophy
Regularly talk to people sincerely about what you believe (TQM). Listen to others' views on this, respond positively to questions on TQM, check out people's understanding. This requires two-way communication – not a lecture! Share your vision.

Visibility and accessibility
Walk the floor regularly – let people know you're there, you are interested and you care. Let people know that their problems are yours. Be aware that this is a high priority item for you and not something to do if you have the time. You fit in other things around this not vice versa.

Be a coach
Be a good communicator, develop coaching skills and use them regularly.

with developing people. It's the manager's job to generate ideas – employees 'do as they're told'.

Constantly look for development opportunities. Help people to find their own answers. Help people to be winners!

Empowering others
Be receptive to others' ideas; there is no such thing as a bad idea. Be expressive and energetic. Ignite people with your freshness and energy. Delegate authority not just duty. Support others when the going gets tough.
Particular skills and behaviour which will be helpful include:
• using people's names;
• knowing your people, their likes, dislikes, family, hobbies, birthdays, anniversaries;
• showing concern when people go sick;
• finding out what people like most/ least about coming to work and doing something about it;
• rewarding people in public;
• disciplining in private;
• sharing the laughter and the sadness;
• smiling;
• rewarding triers as well as winners;
• asking questions more than giving answers;
• being tolerant of mistakes when people are learning or trying something new;
• clarifying and sharing expectations of each other (two-way).

Highlight weaknesses
Let people know what they are not very good at and tell them to pull their socks up.

Build on strengths
Everyone has strengths – recognize them and share this recognition. Provide opportunities for using and developing these strengths. There is

	no such thing as a weakness – only areas for improvement. Be aware of these, share this awareness and develop skill appropriately.
Accountability is the manager's	**Accountability is shared** People need to know and feel that they own and are responsible for their own work. Accountability must be shared and the areas of accountability need to be explicit.
Self-Esteem Self-esteem is power-based. My authority and my position are important to me.	**Self-Esteem** Leaders' self-esteem comes from supporting and nurturing others and feeling good about this process and its benefits.
Managing This is about control and authority.	**TQM** TQM means leading and serving the employee as they are customers too.
Fundamental beliefs (authoritarian) 'Sticks and Carrots'.	**Fundamental beliefs (humanist)** It is important to listen to people. It is important that I accept people's perceptions and feelings and respond to their needs, based on what would help them to feel good as opposed to what would make me feel good.
Trust Give 'em an inch and they'll take a mile.	**Trust** We must trust each other.

The Production Process

Production Production is hierarchically structured with: external suppliers; managers; workers; external customers.	**Production** Production is a process based on a supplier/customer relationship.
Emphasize speed and flexibility	**Emphasize speed and flexibility** ie, to be responsive to change.

The manager is responsible	Everyone is responsible for TQM
The business should be forward-looking	The business must be forward -looking
Believes in directing and controlling	Believes in managing the process
Improvement is important but often difficult to measure	Believes in constantly measuring for improvement
	Improvement We can continually improve the process and reduce waste. What we need to do is involve our people because there lie the answers.

Appendix 3
Communication Audit

COMMUNICATION AUDIT

This questionnaire is designed to collect information about communication in the company. Your answers will be confidential and will be used to compile a summary of people's experience of communication in the company.

The questionnaire has five sections:

- Communicating the vision and direction of the business.
- Communication to do your job effectively.
- Communication for decision-making.
- Communicating with your customers and suppliers.
- Communication and management style.

For each statement you should indicate whether you agree strongly; agree; disagree; or disagree strongly.

Sharing the Vision

	agree strongly	agree	disagree	disagree strongly
I understand and accept the vision of the business.				
Managers in the business behave in a way which is consistent with the vision.				
I understand my own part in achieving the vision.				
I understand the image which the company is trying to project.				
I understand the brand images of the various products and services provided to the company's customers.				
I know who the company's customers are.				
I know the quality standards which the company is committed to provide in its products or services.				

I understand the company's commitment to its social responsibilities.			
I understand what the TQM programme is about.			
I understand what TQM means to me personally.			

Understanding the Purpose of my Job and where I Fit

	agree strongly	agree	disagree	disagree strongly
I understand how my job contributes to the business.				
I understand how my job fits in the process of production or provision of a service.				
I am given information about the objectives of the business.				
I am given information about the long- and short-term plans of the business.				
I am given all the information I need to do my job effectively.				
I am told whenever there are likely to be changes which affect my job.				
I am given information I need on time.				
I am given information about other parts of the business.				
The objectives of my department are clear.				
The objectives of my team are clear.				
My objectives are clear.				
My manager is good at communicating what is happening in the business.				
I am kept up-to-date about what is happening in the business.				
I get up-to-date information on how I am performing.				
I get up-to-date information on how my team is performing.				

Participating in Decision-making

	agree strongly	agree	disagree	disagree strongly
I am asked for ideas on how to improve my own job.				
I am encouraged to produce ideas on ways to improve the general efficiency of the business.				
I am consulted on subjects about which I have information and expertise.				
My manager always listens to my ideas.				
When I make a valid point, or put forward an idea, the response is constructive.				
I am consulted on decisions which affect my job.				
I am consulted on decisions which affect my department.				
I feel involved in the decision-making process.				
We have regular team meetings.				
We have regular departmental meetings.				
I am able to influence what is put on the agenda of team or department meetings.				
When my manager runs a meeting I clearly understand its purpose and its outcomes.				
I believe that senior managers in the business are in touch with what people at my level think.				

Establishing Effective Dialogue with Customers and Suppliers

	agree strongly	agree	disagree	disagree strongly
I know who my internal and external customers are.				
I know who my suppliers are.				
I have discussed and agreed the standards of service required by my customers.				
I am able to discuss any problems openly with my customers.				

Information from my customers is accurate and timely.

I meet my customers regularly to discuss plans, progress, problems, etc.

I am able to discuss difficult issues with my customers.

I discuss my requirements with my suppliers.

Information from my suppliers is accurate and timely.

My suppliers openly discuss difficulties with me.

Management Style

	agree strongly	agree	disagree	disagree strongly
Senior management are good communicators.				
My manager is a good communicator.				
I regularly get feedback from my manager on my performance.				
I am able to give my manager feedback on his/her management style.				
I am able to discuss difficult issues with my manager.				
I always know where I stand with my manager.				
My manager knows what I am thinking.				
Conflict between me and my manager is discussed and resolved.				
My manager is a good counsellor.				
I am able to discuss my growth and development with my manager.				
My manager gives me adequate responsibility.				
My manager treats me with dignity and respect.				

My manager is approachable.			
My manager recognizes my efforts.			
I have regular contact with senior managers.			
I am able to raise grievances with my manager without it counting against me in the future.			
My manager generally does what he/she says he/she is going to do.			
I am able to highlight problems without feeling I will be blamed.			
I have a lot of informal contact with my manager.			

Index

Jones, J A G 74

key task allocation 105
Kolb, D A 79

learning agreement
  illustration 77
  objectives 78
learning
  ensuring success 80–83
  experiential cycle 79
listening 45–6

market-based economy 18

non-value-adding activities 114

open questions 47
order-winning criteria, definition 111–13
organizational pyramid
  advantages and disadvantages 89–90
  description 88–9

Pareto analysis 137–8
Pareto, V 137
performance
  measurement guidelines 102
  questionnaire 98
personal change 146–9
Pfeiffer, J W, Jones, J E 79
poor service, implications 113
problem-solving techniques 133–41
process chart, high-level 93–4
process management, description 90–94
process owner, role of 95
progress, measurement 23–31
Pygmalion effect 88–9

quality
  advantages 37
  comparison of 20–22
  cost of 117–20
  definition 20–22
  as determined by the customer 20
  implications 37
  inspectors 28
  trainer skills 43–50
quality improvement projects
  communication 131
  defining symptoms 126–7

definition 122
failure 140–41
implementation 131
proposal form 128
proposal submission 130–31
role of team leader 132–3
six-stage approach 126–31
structure 126
team choice 125
trainer's questions 141
trainer's role 125

Roddick, A 64

skills, measurement 31
solution and effect diagrams 138–40
supplier/customer requirements 101–3, 107

targets, importance of 28
TQM
  advantages and implications 36–7
  definition 16
  getting started 54
  journey or destination? 22–3, 66–7
  measuring training success 59–60
  purpose 18–19
  senior-level involvement 34
  trainer's exercise 41–3
  trainer's questions 38–9
  trainer's role 17–18
TQM and communication 153–5
TQM management style
  characteristics exercise 145
  characteristics of 168–73
TQM people
  characteristics exercise 144
  characteristics questionnaire 165–7
total work effort, equation 114
trainer
  role of 17–18, 40–43
  questions 60
training
  customer-centred 44
  diagnosing needs 75–8
  diagnostic questions 76
  end-of-course review 84
  evaluation 84–5
  measuring success 59–60
  options 78
  process model 74